TWISTED TRUTHS
OF MODERN
DRESSAGE

In memory of my Mother...
and in tribute to her brother, Louis Wegbecher, an uncle
who, as a rider, had such a profound influence on my
teenage years.

Philippe Karl

TWISTED TRUTHS OF MODERN DRESSAGE

A search for
a classical alternative

CADMOS

ACKNOWLEDGEMENTS

To Bea Borelle for her constant encouragement.

Horses used to illustrate this book:
- Odin (Lusitano. Breeder R. BOUZIN)
- Verdi (Lusitano. Breeder J. PEIGNE)
- Enanquim (Lusitano. Breeder D. LAHAYE)
- Sampaio (Oldenburg Stallion. Breeder H. BLANK-JAEGELER)
- Michelangelo (Trakehner Stallion. The VEBELSGRUND Stud. Mr & Mrs ERDSIEK)
- Quiela (Lusitano Stallion. Breeder M. BIRAGHI)
- Tabea (Trakehner mare. Bea BORELLE)
- Moses (Holsteiner-Haflinger crossbred. Wibke KUHL.)

Copyright © 2008 Cadmos Publishing Limited, Richmond, UK
4. Edition 2012
Copyright of original edition © 2006 Cadmos Verlag GmbH, Schwarzenbek, Germany
Original title: Irrwege der modernen Dressur
Design: Ravenstein + Partner, Verden
Typesetting: Nadine Hoenow
Cover Photo: Alain Laurioux
Photographs: Alain Laurioux, Christiane Slawik, Jacques Toffi
Drawings: Philippe Karl
Translation: Andrew Weal
Printed by: Westermann Druck, Zwickau

British Library Cataloguing in Publication Data
A catalogue record of this book is available from the British Library.

Printed in Germany

Illustrations:

Page 23
Nuno Oliveira - © Villalva
Josef Neckermann - © Bürger archives
Liselott Linsenhoff - © Czerny
Richard Wätjen - © Tiedemann
Alois Podhajski - © Kerschner
All other photographs: © Cadmos archives

Page 33
Ludwig Hünersdorf – drawing: Pforr
François Baucher – drawing: Levilly

Page 44
Drawings: Deutsche Reitvorschrift "H. Dv 12/26"

Page 57
Cadmos archives

Page 64
Cadmos archives

Page 65
Cadmos archives

Page 66
Cadmos archives

Page 67
Cadmos archives

Page 79
Cadmos archives

Page 90
Egon von Neindorff - © Schäfer
Ernst Lindenbauer - © Menzendorf
Richard Wätjen - © Tiedemann
All other photographs: Cadmos archives

Page 105
Cadmos archives

Page 126
Bürger archives

Page 151
Cadmos archives

Contents

Foreword

I always enjoy reading Phillipe Karl's texts, especially when illustrated by the author himself, whose pencil manages to perceptively and reliably capture the elegance and correctness of horses. But the pleasure is particularly due to the technical quality of his words that are true to the concepts of the French school at Saumur, whose mission it is to preserve and hand down to future generations this approach to horsemanship.

As a past Ecuyer in the Cadre Noir, Phillipe Karl has successfully participated in this noble task. He has schooled and presented several horses of different breeds, each with their own specialities, but all satisfying the basic requirements of training laid down by General L'Hotte.

Whether with the Lusitanos "Odin" and "Verdi", the Anglo-Arab "Tetra" or other horses that participated in the Ecole Nationale's shows, Phillipe Karl's presentations were always one of the highlights of these Gala evenings.

An exemplary practitioner and a recognised teacher, Phillipe Karl has recently produced a series of films illustrating the school of légèreté. The beautiful images they show supplement the present work. In them we can see horses that are willing, reliable, and calm, whose accomplished schooling is proof of their stable balance. They make you want to ride with finesse. The ease with which they perform can be seen through the "gallant mouth" described by Pluvinel and La Guérinière, the "Abkauen"(seeking the hand) of Seeger and Steinbrecht and the "soft mobility of the jaw" of Baucher and General L'Hotte. Without this, légèreté cannot be complete; and its absence is an infallible indicator of certain problems in the horse's "state of mind and body" as talked about by General Decarpentry.

Relaxation of the jaw, a preliminary to any mise en main (educating of the mouth), opens the door to impulsion, that most essential of luxuries, and is accompanied by a light contact punctuated by pronounced descentes de main (lowering of the hand).

When experts still agreed on a common notion of good and bad, these values were sought by competitors and upheld by judges. This was an auspicious time for academic dressage. Although dominated by Germany, competition was governed by a framework that included all the finesse of this art, and which extended well beyond national borders.

Today, the art of schooling horses has become a sport dominated by economic factors. There are many white knights who denounce these changes.

Phillipe Karl also has a campaign of his own. His actual achievements give weight to his words in an era marked by the predominance of critics whose equestrian virtuosity is dubious at best. His critical study starts with observations, then an analysis of the situation and a proposed alternative. He presents a very relevant view of how dressage competitions could be in comparison with show jumping competitions.

Although some may find his words harsh, the seriousness of the stakes on one hand and the technical rigour, frankness and passion of the author on the other are not really compatible with any diplomatic attempt at compromise.

I wish his efforts every success and hope that this brings with it responsibilities that his horsemanship and ethics allow him to legitimately claim.

General Pierre Durand
Ecuyer en Chef of the Cadre Noir from 1975 to 1984
Director of the French National School of Equitation from 1984 to 1988

Preface

What is dressage? One dictionary gives the following definition:

"A series of processes based on physical and mental pressure used to create conditioned reflexes with the end purpose of using an animal for various tasks."

This is how we train a dog to be a watchdog, to hunt, to rescue people from avalanches or to guide a blind person, or an elephant to haul tree trunks, a seal to balance a ball on its nose or a rabbit to pop out of a hat.

Naturally, we can judge the value of dressage according to its effectiveness and results, but also according to the quality of the means used to achieve it since these can range widely from a fun learning approach, to force, or even brutality or cruelty.

In terms of riding, all riders consciously or subconsciously do dressage, even if they do not admit it. Horses make no distinction between a so-called "dressage" session and any other form of usage. Whenever we use a horse, whatever we do should be considered either a positive or negative act of dressage training because it marks the horse's psyche.

In the broad sense of the term, "dressage" is therefore all of the principles, methods and processes used to optimise the horse's capabilities, whatever the breed and whatever the discipline.

How has the concept of dressage changed over the centuries? In terms of riding, the middleages were limited to an empirical, warlike and often cruel use of the horse.

From the creation of the first academies during the Italian Renaissance, which occurred in the mid sixteenth century onwards, horsemen ceaselessly tried to develop an ideal training approach. Arts and customs became more refined. Equitation tried to distance itself from brutality:

"Time wears away mistakes and polishes the truth." (G de Levis)

Whilst the majority of those living in the seventeenth century were satisfied with the theory of "animals-as-machines", the discordant voice of William Cavendish, 1st Duke of Newcastle laid down one of the founding precepts of classical dressage:

"Art must always follow nature and never oppose it."

In the eighteenth century, the century of enlightenment and encyclopaedists, equitation started to become more rationalised.

François Robichon de la Guérinière contributed brilliantly to this with his School of Horsemanship:

"Knowledge of what is natural in a horse is one of the cornerstones of the art of riding and all horsemen should make it a main point of study... Without this theory, practice is always uncertain."

This philosophy, strengthened by the scientism of the period, is a common thread throughout all equestrian research in the nineteenth century. General L'Hotte, one of the best known students of F. Baucher, wrote the following in 1906 in his book *Equestrian Questions*:

"Nature is the first of all masters. Its book is the fairest, most knowledgeable of all books, the most useful to consult. The effects recorded in its pages lead us to the causes which generate them."

Finally in the 1920s, with the creation of dressage competitions, the art of schooling horses became a sports discipline.

Governed by the International Equestrian Federation, this discipline has become a sports business that is professionalised, sponsored, mediatised and globalised and used as an absolute reference for training purposes.

Since "doubt is a remedy taught by wisdom" (Publius Syrius, Roman writer from the 1st century BC) we can rightly challenge the roots, consequences and historical legitimacy of such a monopoly in comparison with our classical equestrian culture.

Considered as a specialised discipline, dressage only has a meaning if it results from the search for the most correct processes, in other words methods that are both efficient and gentle, because they are not contrary to the horse's nature.

In this book, we propose an analysis of modern dressage based on knowledge of the horse. This is the most reliable approach to avoid the pitfalls of fashion, the inevitable restrictiveness of specialisation, the preconceived ideas of different schools and the tyranny of current dogmas.

Using fundamental data on anatomy, physiology, locomotion, balance, psychology and the all-too-neglected science of common sense, we will embark on a point-by-point study of the principles that govern official dressage. We will take these principles from dressage manuals and more particularly from those of the German Equestrian Federation, the current bible for any rider who rides in a rectangle surrounded by letters… wherever he is on the planet. The official handbooks of the German National Equestrian Federation, the Kenilworth Press published by, are Book 1: *The Principles of Riding*, completely revised edition 1997, and Book 2: *Advanced Techniques of Riding*, edition 1996. (These are referred to throughout the text as B1 and B2.)

In light of this analysis we will reveal the shortcomings and explain the detrimental consequences of the dogmas of modern dressage. This will also allow us to deduce well thought-out alternatives on the following aspects:
• definitions of major equestrian concepts
• dressage methods
• rider education
• teacher training
• criteria used to judge dressage competitions and the design of the tests themselves.

Lastly, our equestrian culture requires that we should look at the writings of the best known masters to confirm the legitimacy of what we propose.

"Correct and incorrect do not result from nature, but from the law."
(Milesian school of philosophy, VIth century BC)

*The horse is
the best all masters.*

KEY ISSUES
IN DRESSAGE

Checkmate...by the horse!

Riding in general, and dressage in particular, involve a certain number of key issues that we need to identify.

They cannot be effectively dealt with unless we make the right diagnosis.

Psychological Aspects

Analysis

In the past few years, under the pressure of ethologists and other "horse whisperers", dressage manuals have consented to include a few pages on the psychological aspects of riding.

In Book 1, "*The Principles of Riding*", we are judiciously reminded of the main traits of a "horse's nature" by the following general recommendations:

> "*The schooling of a horse cannot only be judged on the quality of its paces under the rider, but also the maintaining of its natural attitude and personality. It is these fulfilled horses, ready to give the best of themselves in their daily work, that produce a stable and harmonious relationship between man and his horse. These foundations will be strengthened and developed through patience, a sense of psychology and frequent reward.*"
>
> "*In riding, progress relies on theoretical knowledge. Knowledge of the nature and behaviour of horses, how to look after them as well as of riding and dressage principles are naturally essential for any serious and responsible horseman.*" *(B1, page 12)*

We can only agree with such statements. But a dressage manual cannot simply rely on declarations of intent, however admirable they are. Without decrees for application or resources for implementation, a law is no more than a hollow shell. Preaching the benefits of equine knowledge is a good idea, but it is even better to say what you need to know and to draw some real conclusions and rules that can be used to guide dressage riders.

The basics of equine psychology allow us to determine three main stages in the relationship between rider and horse.

The taming stage

Even when raised close to man, a horse naturally remains a herbivore with a gregarious instinct and with a highly developed sense of hierarchy. Since it is a victim of predators in the wild, the horse is fearful and has very sharp senses, using flight to save its skin.

To satisfy his needs, man subjects the horse to a way of life that is contrary to its nature, separating it from its fellow creatures and imposing worrying situations on it, starting with the bit and the saddle.

Nothing good is possible until the horse accepts that man is a well-meaning and dominant fellow creature.

Trust and relaxation are absolute preconditions for any work of quality. In real terms this means banishing any use of force and coercion, as well as any constraining devices.

"The free consent of the horse gives better results than any remedies through which we try to constrain him."
(Salomon de la Broue)

"Of all the conditioning required to educate a horse, the most important is that of his will." *(Charles-Hubert Raabe)*

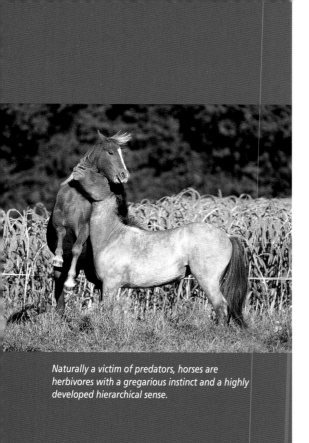

Naturally a victim of predators, horses are herbivores with a gregarious instinct and a highly developed hierarchical sense.

To satisfy his needs, man subjects the horse to a way of life that is contrary to its nature.
Photos: Laurioux

The learning stage

Horses are not just a mass of muscles to be shaped in order to satisfy our desires or to produce a performance, they are sensitive beings. Expressions such as: "The horse must do this... the horse must give that" are all too common in dressage jargon. The horse owes us nothing, it is we who have a duty to make ourselves understood.

"It is essential to link the rider's gestures to those of the horse; this link is none other than the horse's intelligence together with his moral consent."
(Maurice Hontang, "Psychologie du cheval")

So what is this intelligence worth? No master based their dressage approach more on the intelligence of the horse than François Baucher:

"Horses have perception as well as feeling, comparison and memory; they therefore have judgement and recall, and they therefore have intelligence."

And we can believe that this approach is justified since General Decarpentry wrote the following in *Baucher and His School:*

"The results obtained by Baucher were extraordinary from all points of view. However it would seem that the speed with which he obtained them is what is most remarkable - it was truly prodigious."

In fact, horses are capable of understanding everything that the rider is capable of getting them to understand.

In the end, it is the rider who needs a high level of equestrian intelligence in order to get the best out of the horse.

How does a horse learn? Fearful and worried by nature, horses spend most of their time assessing potential dangers in their environment. Any new element will monopolise their attention and is assessed on the basis of their past experience.

A brutal, authoritarian or simply clumsy rider, focuses the horse's attention by unwittingly becoming an aggressor. He triggers protective mechanisms (tension, resistances, evasions) which hinder or cancel out any quality learning.

For a rider to achieve significant and quick progress from a horse, he must have a subtle teaching strategy that takes account of the horse's psychological traits, its anatomy, essential points of its locomotion and the laws of balance.

We often insist on the importance of patience. But it is powerless on its own. It would be better to say:
Patience is not a science
But one needs...
a lot of science and a lot of patience.

The skill of a rider lies in the way that he plans a logical sequence of learning events. The wiser he is, the more he will arouse the horse's curiosity and provide an element of fun in work that it enjoys.

Typical learning sequence

A rider communicates with his horse via the "aids". Therefore, he above all teaches a language that is intended to influence the horse's movements. Several steps must be complied with in a consistent learning sequence in order to ensure success.

1. The language of the aids
Ensure that the horse understands all of the necessary aids for what you want to teach him.

2. Objective
Determine the smallest possible step in progress, relative to what the horse already knows. Any demands that are inconsistent or excessive will be seen as aggressive.

3. Prepare
Focus the horse's attention on exercises that favourably bring together the conditions for the coming experience.

4. Assess
Put the horse in the new situation (position, balance, locomotion) in which it will naturally and certainly react, even if it is only by very slightly starting to do the desired behaviour.

5. Reward
Immediately reward the horse to confirm that this is what you want (use your voice, pat the horse, let him rest, give him a treat, etc.).

"You must reward the slightest concession as if it was a full submission, because it will certainly lead directly to that." *(Alexandre Guérin, 1817–1884)*

To do well, we need knowledge.
To teach well, we need understanding

6. Repeat
By repeating the "assess" step and its reward we confirm, fix and perfect the new behaviour.

As a necessary to acquire any knowledge, repetition often leads the horse to respond by anticipation during the preparatory sequence.

This behaviour is a sign of goodwill and enthusiasm and the horse should never be punished for this. On the other hand, you must frequently repeat the preparation step and maintain it without executing the response.

This result should be rewarded just as much as a perfect response. In this way the horse learns to remain attentive to the rider and wait for a request that may come – or not as the case may be.

7. Perfect
As the new behaviour becomes imprinted in the horse's mind, we can reduce the preparation step and depend more on decisive aiding.

In the end, the aids themselves will suffice and will become increasingly discreet until they are virtually invisible.

It then looks like the rider simply has to think about a movement for the horse to do it. This expresses the myth of the centaur.

8. Review
Something that is learned is only of value if it is part of a consistent whole, enhancing previous steps and used as a reference for future experiences.

The practising stage

When well designed, the learning phase is much shorter (sometimes a few lessons) than the period of physical adaptation necessary to correctly execute something (at least a few months).

Frequent and daily repetition is therefore essential for the muscles and joints to be able to perfect the movement, but this is not without its pitfalls.

Indeed whilst the learning phase arouses the horse's attention because it is new, the repetitive nature of the practising phase tends to bore the horse and cause distraction. It produces mechanical and subconscious responses, like a child who can repeat a lesson he has learned by heart without really thinking about it.

This is what we call a "drilled" horse.

To avoid this pitfall riders must take a certain number of precautions:

• Vary figures, diversifying sequences of exercises, changing situations, changing contexts and locations, with the sole purpose of maintaining the horse's interest in its work.
• Avoid repeating and prolonging an exercise or an air without any purpose. "Kilometric" dressage tends to physically wear out the horse, anaesthetise its attention and dull its intelligence.

Do not confuse dressage with bodybuilding.

Show yourself to be creative rider with a good imagination. Never limit your work to presentation objectives. Hacking, outside work and jumping are irreplaceable gymnastic exercises for the body and mind. Never lose sight of the risks involved in too restrictive an approach to any specialisation… including dressage.

Conclusion

Dressage competitions inherently promote repetative and drilling. Riders can repeat the same tests as much as they want in the ethereal and purified environment of the dressage arena.

This is why, when taken to extremes, "dressage" horses do not behave like "schooled" horses… and can be unable to bear the slightest unplanned event, sometimes performing rather embarrassing flights of fantasy for their "passengers" (over-excited, run-away piaffe during a prize giving, bolting during the lap of honour, etc.).

What is the purpose of a discipline in which submission is a goal in itself or when it creates difficulties for specialists in situations where any enlightened amateur leisure rider would have no problems?

> Imagine the result for showjumping, both for the work of horses and the interest of the public, if the events were always held on identical courses and show-grounds: same jumps, same sizes and same distances? It would be a disaster.

Suggestions

We could consider a competition in which each level of rider knows what exercises and airs are on the programme, but never knows either the figures or the sequences for the tests on that day.

A skilful jury would determine a dressage test that is pinned up like a showjumping course… at the last moment. The test would, of course, be read out to the rider.

This competitive concept would assess and empower the judges, increase the interest of the public, protect the horses from a dull training programme, put those who rely on intensive last minute practising firmly in their place (even if they have better horses) and encourage well-founded dressage methods and intelligent riders (even when they are riding average horses).

> Dressage competitions could be improved by redesigning them to really take account of the nature of horses.

Natural Crookedness

"On the left side, the neck muscles are stiff, contracted and refuse to release. This is considered the stiff side. However, the difficult side is the right, hollow side.

The right-hind escapes to the right, the horse pushes against the rider's right leg and refuses the contact on the right rein. The aim of the work will be to bring this hind leg to engage under the body. Straightness must always be achieved by aligning the forehand with the hindquarters and not the other way round.

For example, if the horse's haunches escape to the right, the rider must stop this tendency by acting with his right leg. His left leg, close to the girth, will increase the engagement of the left hind. The left hand must be kept low, with the left rein containing and controlling the left shoulder, whilst the right hand brings the forehand to the right until there is alignment of the right-fore with the right-hind."

(FN Guidlines for Riding and Driving, German Equestrian Federation vol. 1, p. 147.)

This diagnosis is very superficial. It omits the deep rooted causes and their major consequences, those involving balance.

The approach falls short in two respects: it deals with the effects rather than the causes, and it supposes that the horse is already well advanced in its schooling; however the problem appears from the start.

We can look at this in more detail.

Causes

Foals are crooked from birth due to the foetal position that they grow in: shorter on one side than the other. Not all horses are bent to the right, far from it. Whether due to genetics or to chance, does not really matter, statistically the proportion is something like 50-50%.

Nature seems to be more inventive than the dressage manuals.

But never mind! We can take the case of a horse which is hollow to the right and analyse the causes and consequences of this crookedness. This will give us information on how we should approach this in our work.

• The deep rooted and original cause resides in the natural bend of the neck to the right. The main cervical ligament is shifted to the right and the mane falls to the right. The horse tends to carry its head to the right and tends to weight its left shoulder to compensate.

• Since the bending of the neck has an impact on the rest of the spine, in movement periodic dorso-lumbar waves produce bends, of greater amplitude to the right than to the left. Consequently the horse's haunches escape to the right.

• Therefore the right hind is more advanced than the left hind, but it escapes to the side. It reaches more than it pushes.

As opposed to this, the left hind is in a position to provide the majority of propulsion, but its engagement remains limited.

> "Like man, horses come into the world with two different sides, one strong and the other weak."
>
> *(Commandant Jean-Charles Licart)*

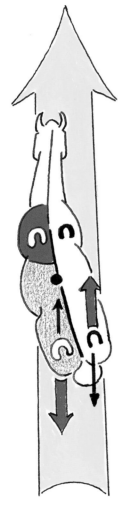

Consequences natural crookedness: a horse that is hollow to the right, has its haunches that escape to the right and weights its left lateral pair.

• In movement, the inert parts of the body (thoracic and abdominal) move more to the left than to the right. This naturally increases the weighting of the left lateral pair.

• Overall, the whole spine is bent to the right, especially the neck. The horse relieves the weight on its shortened right lateral pair (concave side) and weights its open left lateral pair (convex side).

Impact on our work

• The horse turns comfortably to the right and tends to enlarge the curves through its shoulders by bending its neck to the right.

• Conversely, to the left, the horse turns short, falling on the inside shoulder with its head carried to the outside.

• The horse canters more easily on the right leg, but with its haunches in. It is not uncommon for the horse to disunite its hind legs when cantering on a circle to the left.

What the rider feels

• The horse is willing to take a contact on the left rein whereas it refuses to take a contact on the right.

• The rider's seat drops more to the right than to the left on each stride and his right leg is nearer to the horse's hindquarters (concavity to the right) whereas his left leg tends to be pushed away from the left hindquarters (convexity on the left).

• Since the horse weights its left shoulder and advances its right hind more, if the rider is not careful the horse will automatically trot on the left diagonal in rising trot.

• In lateral work, the horse will be more willing to move its shoulders to the left and its haunches to the right.

• In all work on the right rein, the horse seems flexible and "balanced", on the left rein it seems to be stiff and "out of balance".

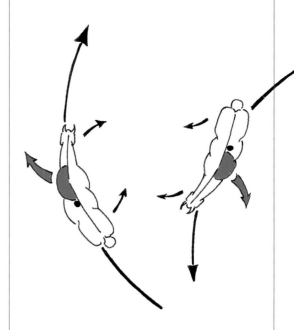

When turning to the right, a horse which is hollow to the right tends to enlarge the curve through its shoulders. To the left it turns short and falls on its inside shoulder.

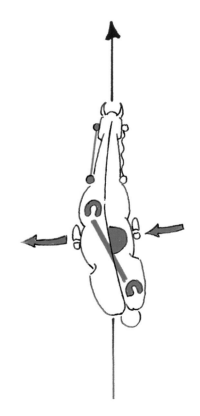

A horse that is hollow to the right tends to lean on the left rein and carry the left diagonal further forward than the right diagonal. The rider's seat drops more to the right than to the left, his right leg is more nearer to the horse's hindquarters and his left leg tends to be pushed away from them.

The search for straightness

Rectifying this crookedness is one of the main and priority objectives of training since the correct functioning of the locomotor system and the physical health of the horse in the long term depend on an even distribution of forces.

The question is: what education to the aids and which gymnastic exercises can we use to seek straightness? A good gymnastics teacher would not simply order you to "hold yourself straight!" He would put you through a series of exercises intended to compensate for your crookedness: stretching the shortened muscles and strengthening the elongated muscles to gradually correct your posture.

In the same way, with the horse's activity level compatible with relaxation, the rider will alternate work on both reins that is designed to reverse the horse's posture and imbalances. An effective gymnastics approach will compensate for nature without being contrary to it.

Since the neck is at the root of the problem, the rider will use this wonderful point of balance and leverage to straighten and rebalance the front end to benefit the whole horse. A horse that resists the left rein, has shorter muscles on the right side of the neck which refuse to lengthen. If there is truly stiffness, then it is on the right side and not the left side.

"The main pitfall in training is to focus on the effects rather than searching for, and changing, the causes." *(Etienne Beudant)*

Therefore, we can see that only pronounced and repeated bending of the whole neck to the left can correct this problem. The rider will use this, notably to shift the weight towards the right shoulder, therefore lightening the left side (N.B.: people who train horses to lie down have to start by putting one shoulder on the ground. They only manage this by bending the neck fully in the opposite direction. This confirms the fact that, in terms of balance, it is the neck and the shoulders which are important).

In the end, this means teaching the horse to hold itself to the right in the same way as it spontaneously does to the left, which fully justifies educating the horse to respond to a "neck-rein" (a rein effect that is used in all types of riding where the rider only uses one hand).

In later work, a slight bend to the left together with the left rein pressing on the neck will be enough to bring the shoulders in front of the haunches.

Popular wisdom says:

"What is complicated is unimportant, and what is important is never complicated."

The rider then has to focus on harmonising the way the hind legs move, by controlling the haunches. He will pay particular attention to positions that encourage engagement of the left hind, as well as those that stop the right hind from escaping and that involve it more in propulsion.

Lateral work will be particularly useful in this with the following focus:

• shoulder-in… to the right with limited bend and a pronounced angle… to the left with a pronounced bend and limited angle
• travers… to the left with pronounced bend and a pronounced angle… to the right with limited bend and a limited angle
• renvers… on a circle to the right with pronounced bend and angle… to the left with limited bend and angle
• rein back on circles to the left with a distinct inward bend.

The horse will gradually acquire a more balanced ability to cross, push and engage with

Horses that are hollow to the right have muscles on the right side of the neck that are shorter and harder to stretch.

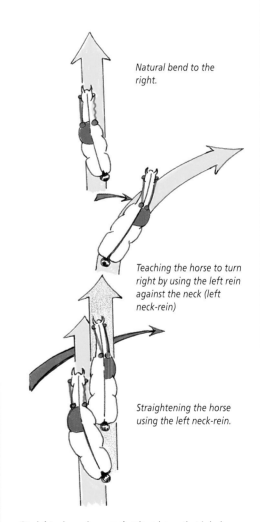

Natural bend to the right.

Teaching the horse to turn right by using the left rein against the neck (left neck-rein)

Straightening the horse using the left neck-rein.

Straightening using a neck-rein: *a horse that is hollow to the right must firstly learn to push its weight to the right shoulder under the action of the left rein against the neck to turn him towards the right in a counter-bend. Following this, a slight bend to the left together with the left rein against the neck will be sufficient to straighten the horse.*

both hind legs which will lead to the straightening of the dorso-lumbar segment.

Conclusion

All of this work carried out firstly at walk, then at trot and lastly at canter will be a minimum requirement for the rider to claim that he has a straight horse… which means: a horse that is symmetrical due to the equal flexibility-mobility of the left and right sides.

"Through the perfection of his art, a horseman will spend his whole life correcting this imperfection."
(Jacques d'Auvergne, 1729–1798)

Therefore, you do not "hold" a horse "straight", unless you content yourself with a very approximate approach to managing stiffness using "tricks".

Straightness is not possible to impose on a horse. It is the result of a lot of systematic work involving suppling and mobilisation in every direction.

By recommending that people ride a young horse "forwards and straight", we are asking for the impossible and causing riders to cover more kilometres and resort to expedients rather than educating a horse to the aids using a corrective gymnastic approach, thus leading to a lot of work for nothing.

It would be a better idea to suggest working the horse to that it is:

• above all relaxed, without which the exercise has no value
• driven forwards, because without impulsion there is no horsemanship, but always within the limit that maintains relaxation
• flexible, to harmonise the horse's forces and therefore work towards straightness

This is summarised in General L'Hotte's well-known formula: "calm, forwards, straight",

having stated elsewhere that dressage must "… combine impulsion with the flexibility of springs".

Balance

With four legs and a strong instinct for self-preservation, a horse normally manages to stay upright… often in spite of its rider. Therefore, in the basic sense of the word it always remains "in balance". In dressage this can give a feeling of impunity that the rider is all too willing to take as confirmation of his theories (even if they are contrary to the horse's nature) and his approaches (even if they are absurd). However, when jumping, the sanctions are immediately visible, objective and sometimes painful. They are undeniable and impossible to wrap in hollow words. This leads to the dressage world eruditely using the terms "on the forehand", "in a horizontal balance" or "on the haunches" without rhyme or reason.

In riding, the search for postures which provide an "optimum balance" for a given movement is one of the keys of any intelligent dressage approach… since we cannot escape the universal effect of gravity with impunity. It is rather surprising to notice that the dressage manuals remain evasive and even silent on such an important point.

Natural balance

Built for flight and speed, a horse is naturally balanced on its forehand. All experiments to measure the weighting of the forelegs (Wf) and the hindlegs (Wh) carried out by General Morris or Captain de Saint-Phalle amongst others, have revealed a weighting coefficient (WC) for the forehand calculated in the following way:

$$1/10 < WC = \frac{W_f - W_h}{W_f + W_h}$$

We will take the average value equal to 1/9. In addition, the weight of the rider is distributed as follows:

	Forelegs	Hindlegs
Rider sitting	2/3	1/3
Rider on the stirrups	4/5	1/5

Example:
Horse weighing 450kg rider weighing 75kg

	W_f	W_h
Horse	250	200
Rider sitting	50	25
Total	300	225

The forelegs are subject to an extra load of 75kg or in other words 1/7 of the total weight. This is enormous.

Once in the saddle, a rider can only hope to optimise his use of a horse if he remains in perfect control of the horse's balance.

Initially the rider has to manage the horse's natural balance as best as he can by putting the horse in as comfortable a situation as possible. We will come back to this.

Then, the main focus of his work will involve gradual gymnastic exercises intended to produce a more equitable weight distribution between the forehand and the hindquarters. Only an "unstable balance" can give immediate mobility in every direction. From this point of view a rider can be compared to a tightrope walker.

The equestrian concept of collection corresponds to this search for an "unstable balance".

We can even say that riding itself can be boiled down to our ability to modify the horse's balance at will.

Collection

How can we achieve this "unstable balance" that we need for mobility and ease? By lifting the base of the neck, bringing it more vertically above the forelegs and by shortening the weight-bearing base.

• **Lifting the base of the neck.**
Experiments carried out by General Morris and F. Baucher gave the following results:

• Maximum lifting of the neck, with the head in front of the vertical: shifting back of 1/20th of the mass.
• Lifting of the neck combined with flexing of the poll; ramener position: shifting back of 1/25th of the mass.
• Extending the neck: 1/25th more on the forehand.

We can apply these figures to the example given above: a 450kg horse and a 75kg rider sitting in the saddle.

450kg Horse 75kg Rider	W_f	W_h	Difference	Weighting coefficient WC
Horse standing freely	300	225	75	1/7
Extension of the neck (+ 1/25 ± 18kg)	309	216	93	1/5.6
Lifting without poll flexion (- 1/20 ± -22.5kg)	288.75	236.25	52.5	1/10
Lifting with poll flexion (- 1/25 ± - 18kg)	291	234	57	1/9

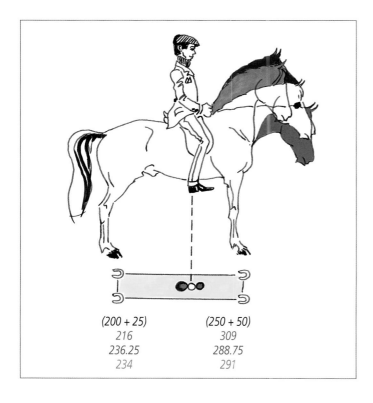

(200 + 25)   (250 + 50)
216   309
236.25   288.75
234   291

Distribution of weight between the forehand and the hindquarters varies according to the position of the horse's head and neck. The figures give the weight carried by the forelegs and hindlegs in four different positions.

We can draw the following conclusions from this:

• The presence of a rider greatly affects the balance of the horse, with the weighting coefficient increasing from 1/9 to 1/7.
• Extending the neck increases the weight on the forehand: WC = 1/5.6
• Lifting the base of the neck significantly shifts the centre of gravity since, with flexing of the poll, the WC is decreased to 1/9. The imbalance generated by the rider is therefore cancelled out and the horse gets back its natural balance – a noticeable difference! Without poll flexion, the WC is reduced to 1/10th and the horse slightly improves its natural balance – maybe enough to quell the passion of those who swear by extreme poll flexion.

Having said that, whilst lifting the neck is necessary to rebalance the horse, it is not enough to achieve an unstable balance.

• **Shortening of the weight-bearing base.**
It is basically in piaffe that a horse shows its ability to work on a shortened weight-bearing base. We can have a look at how the balance varies according to changes in the weight-bearing base. We can go back and look at the case of a horse weighing 450kg, ridden in the "Ramener" position (lifted neck and flexed poll) by a rider weighing 75kg, a sitting in the saddle:

• Basis: perpendicular plumb line of the supporting diagonal pair
• Dh: distance from the point at which the hind leg touches the ground to the plumb line of the centre of gravity
• Df: the same for the foreleg
• WC: weighting coefficient of the forelegs
• Wf: weight on the forelegs
• Wh: weight on the hindlegs

Sketch	Basis	D_h/D_f	WC	W_f (kg)	W_h (kg)	Weighting
0	Natural limb position with ramener	5/4	1/9	291	234	
						+ 57 kg on the forehand
1	Shortening Fore: 1 Hind: 0	5/3	2/8	328	197	
						+ 131 kg on the forehand
2	Shortening Fore: 1 Hind: 1	4/3	1/7	300	225	
						+ 75 kg on the forehand
	with overbending			315	210	
						+ 105 kg on the forehand
3	Shortening Fore: 2 Hind: 1	4/2	2/6	350	175	
						+ 175 kg on the forehand
	with overbending			365	160	
						+ 205 kg on the forehand
4	Shortening Fore: 0 Hind: 1	4/4	0	262,5	262,5	
						0 kg = "horizontal balance"
5	Shortening Fore: 0 Hind: 2	3/4	–(1/7)	225	300	
						+ 75 kg on the hindquarters "on the haunches"
6 7	Shortening Fore: 0 Hind: 3	2/4	–(2/6)	175	350	
						+ 175 kg on the haunches "approaching a pesade"

We can deduce the following:

- **1** – Bringing the forelegs under the horse puts it on the forehand (+ 131kg)
- **2** – Even with an equivalent engagement of the hindquarters, bringing the forelegs under the horse puts the horse on the forehand (+ 75kg). The overbent attitude is halfway between the natural posture and an extension of the neck and increases the weighting of the forehand by around 30kg. In this situation the extra weighting of the forelegs reaches 105kg.
- **3** – Overbending encourages the horse to bring its forelegs back and pushes the centre of gravity forward.
Under these conditions, the extra weighting of the forehand can reach 205kg.
- **4** – Balance is only improved if the weight bearing foreleg remains vertical whilst the hindquarters engage. The horse is then in a "horizontal balance".
This expression is used wrongly to designate a horse in a lengthened frame. In this case its silhouette may well be horizontal, but its balance is not. A horizontal balance is a minimum condition for a correct piaffe.
- **5** – Beyond a horizontal balance the horse is really "on the haunches" or "uphill". These are the conditions required for a genuine piaffe: with the haunches lowered and with all the joints flexed from the back to the hocks, the horse can propel itself upwards bearing less weight on its shoulders. It jumps from one diagonal to the other as if free of gravity (N.B.: the natural balance is now reversed).
- **6 & 7** – Going even further, the horse sits even more on its haunches.
As the weight moves back, the horse gradually sits on the hindquarters and approaches a pesade.

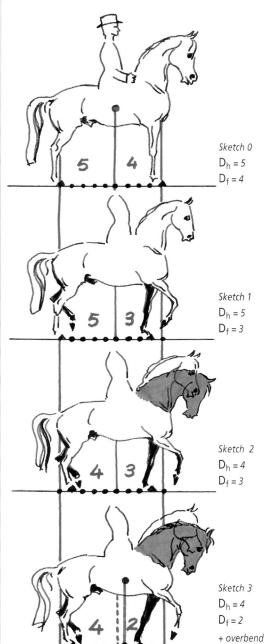

Sketch 0
$D_h = 5$
$D_f = 4$

Sketch 1
$D_h = 5$
$D_f = 3$

Sketch 2
$D_h = 4$
$D_f = 3$

Sketch 3
$D_h = 4$
$D_f = 2$
+ overbend

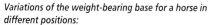

Variations of the weight-bearing base for a horse in different positions:
D_h designates the distance from where the hindleg comes into contact with the ground to the plumb-line of the centre of gravity (in whatever units), Df is the same distance for the foreleg. The first drawing shows a horse standing naturally in a ramener position. In cases 1 to 3, the horse shortens the weight bearing base to different extents using the forelegs and the hindlegs. Drawing 3 also shows the shifting forward of the centre of gravity in an overbent horse.

This sketch shows the weighting of the forelegs according to the different positions of the head and neck.

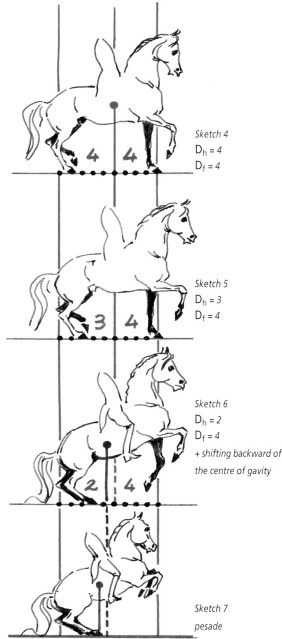

Sketch 4
$D_h = 4$
$D_f = 4$

Sketch 5
$D_h = 3$
$D_f = 4$

Sketch 6
$D_h = 2$
$D_f = 4$
+ shifting backward of the centre of gavity

Sketch 7
pesade

In cases 4 to 7, the horse shortens its weight-bearing base only by increasing engagement of the hindlegs under its body – to a point where all of its weight is over the haunches and the horse lifts into a pesade.

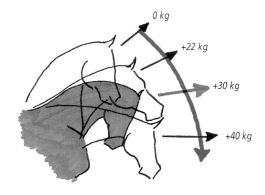

0 kg

+22 kg

+30 kg

+40 kg

Conclusion

The piaffe results from a raising of the forehand with the weight-bearing foreleg remaining vertical… and a lowering of the haunches with distinct and active engagement of the hindlegs under the body. A genuine piaffe is therefore excellent proof of both balance and impulsion… a sign of accomplished schooling.

However, in "top level" competition we regularly see horses winning with a "piaffe" that has the forelegs coming well under, with a low poll, hindlegs that are scarcely engaged or not engaged at all, and the forelegs moving with very little elevation. (Without mentioning gait irregularities, ataxic gaits, swishing tails and grinding teeth.) These "piaffes" correspond to cases 1, 2 and 3. They put the horse more on its shoulders than before it had done any dressage at all. This is anti-collection: a perversion of balance that leads to a complete distortion of a fundamental classical air. And yet these are outstanding horses ridden by dressage professionals: flagrant proof of failure which discredits all of their work and which should be unacceptable!

How can we explain the promotion of such poor imitations?

• Either we admit that "collection" is no longer an objective of dressage competition…
• Or that judges do not know what a genuine piaffe really is…
• Or lastly, that they are complicit in a system that is in a state of cultural failure, whilst being powerful and lucrative.

In the end, there is one certainty: the big losers in this business are riding in general and the horses in particular.

False piaffes

Today we regularly see "top level" competition winners on horses that "piaffe" leaning over their forelegs, with a low poll, hindquarters that are scarcely engaged or not engaged at all, and front legs without any elevation.
These sketches were based on photos showing top level riders of various nationalities.

Otto Lörke

General Decarpentry

Etienne Beudant

Nuno Oliveira

Josef Neckermann

Liselott Linsenhoff

Richard Wätjen

Alois Podhajsky

Otto Lörke

True piaffes

Piaffe is excellent proof of balance and impulsion and is a sign of accomplished schooling. It results in the raising of the forehand, with the weight-bearing foreleg remaining vertical and a lowering of the haunches with distinct and active engagement of the hindquarters under the body. The photo on the bottom right shows Otto Lörke in a pesade, an air in which the horse shifts all of its weight back towards the rear and ends up on its hindquarters.

Please note: all of these horses have their head distinctly in front of the vertical and their poll the highest point.

An unschooled horse reacts to the rider's weight and the tension in the reins by hollowing to a degree. This posture corresponds to a shortening of the top-line muscles and an extending of the bottom-line muscles.

Gymnastic Approach

Generally, a young unschooled horse reacts to the rider's weight and the tension in the reins by hollowing to a degree. The poll opens, the neck hollows, the withers drop and the haunches trail behind, to varying extents. This posture corresponds to a shortening of the top line muscles and a stretching of the bottom-line muscles. All of which is a long way from the roundness we need for collection.

In gymnastic terms this is the first problem to be solved, since supple extension of the top line is the cornerstone of a correctly schooled horse. Collection or good jumping style depends on this.

Observation

Today, virtually all dressage specialists drop the poll and bring the head behind the vertical to make the horse go "round" and make it "give its back". By copying these "champions", both teachers and beginners are all overbending their horses.

This deserves some in-depth study.

The champions of overbending:
Today, virtually all dressage specialists lower the horse's poll and bring its head behind the vertical, some to an extreme degree. These photos were taken in the warm-up ring at international competitions. Photos: Toffi

The consequences of overbending

• Cervical ligaments
The upper ligaments are subject to extreme and prolonged stretching, leading to tearing of fibres, separation at the insertions, inflammation, etc.
The neck is bent sharply in the middle and loses its muscle tone.

• Parotid glands
These are subject to extreme compression without any adaptive process, which leads to their gradual distortion. Very painful inflammation and irreversible induration are frequently the consequence.

• The eye and the ear
The following information is taken from the remarkable book by Dominique Olivier La Vérité sur L'équilibre (*The Truth about Balance*) (Editions Belin). In order to adjust its posture and adapt its movement to all requirements of balance, just like man, the horse has three points of reference:

• The ground- of which it has a tactile perception through its feet. It coordinates its movements to maintain the mass above the weight-bearing points.
• The environment- that horses understand through their vision, assessing everything at a distance and therefore anticipating their reactions. However, we know that the binocular visual field of the horse only has a very limited angle and it can only see a long way when its head is lifted high, with the poll open (alert posture).

• Once the horse is overbent it only has limited sideways monocular vision and binocular vision that only just allows it to see where it is putting its feet. It is made to move blindly, or almost.

Thus separated from their environment in this way, this is why many of these horses lose all expression and look as though they are autistic.
• Gravity- which is perceived by the inner ear. This has three "semi-circular canals" placed perpendicularly to one another that allow the horse to situate itself in three dimensional space. Moreover these canals have sensors which record vertical, horizontal and lateral accelerations.

All of this tactile, visual and gravitational information is processed by the brain. However, in extreme situations, like other species, the horse stabilises its head in one position that optimises the functioning of this navigation system: this is why trotting, flat racing and show jumping horses set the axis of their head at around 30° in front of the vertical.

Dominique Olivier concludes on this subject with the following: Taking the horse a long way from its natural reference position for long periods of time and adding the loss of its visual points of reference will very probably cause balance disorders (conflicting situations between the points of reference). Whilst the experimental study of these phenomena has not been carried out for horses, they are well known in man (sea sickness is an example) and many animal species.

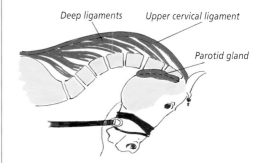

The upper ligaments of an overbent horse are subject to extreme and prolonged extension that causes lesions. The parotid glands are subject to extreme compression.

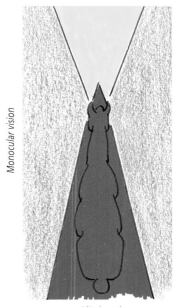

The binocular field of vision in a horse only operates in a very limited angle (shown in yellow) and only extends for ahead when the horse's head is positioned high with the poll open. Once it is overbent the horse only has restricted binocular vision that scarcely allows him to judge where it is putting its feet.

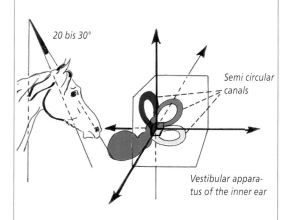

20 bis 30°

Semi circular canals

Vestibular appara-tus of the inner ear

The "navigation system" of the inner ear allows the horse to keep its balance. It only works optimally if the head axis has an angle of 20-30° to the vertical. (Taken from The Truth on Balance *by Dominique Olivier)*

In an overbent horse, the brachio-cephalic muscles on both sides of the neck are shortened and contracted to the extreme, which blocks the movement of the shoulders and causes the horse to shift its weight over its forelegs and come under in front. In addition overbending hinders lateral flexion of the neck.

Brachio-cephalic muscles

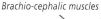

In this position the "navigation system" of the inner ear can no longer function properly.
Photo: Toffi

In extreme situations the horse stabilises its head in a position that optimises the operation of this navigation system: this explains the characteristic head carriage, with the poll angle open, of the trotting horse ...

... and of the flat racing horse.
Photos: Laurioux

• **Brachio-cephalic muscles**

These are the muscles connecting the head to the foreleg, which are shortened and contracted in the extreme. This blocks the movement of the shoulders, which are also overloaded. The horse tends to shift its weight over its forelegs and come under in front. We have seen the consequences in terms of collected work!

In addition, overbending results in a bilateral shortening of the brachio-cephalic muscles that is incompatible with lateral flexion of the neck.

This excludes lateral suppling and precludes the movement of the head and neck to balance vertebral swinging related to locomotion.

Since overbending results in bilateral shortening of the brachio-cephalic muscles, it also means that an overbent horse will have great difficulty in bending its neck to the side.
Photo: Toffi

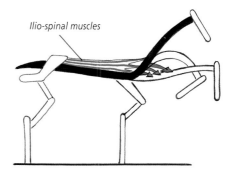

Ilio-spinal muscles

The ilio-spinal muscles link the hips to the spine at the base of the neck. They can only stretch if the latter extends horizontally.

• **Ilio-spinal muscles**

These are back muscles that connect the hips to vertebrae at the base of the neck. They can only be lengthened by extending the base of the neck horizontally.

However, overbending results in extreme flexion of the front part of the neck (stretching the splenius and complexus) and blocking its base (not affecting the ilio-spinal muscles).

Has anyone ever seen a horse overbend itself to jump in order to bascule better and use its back more? On the contrary, it stretches its nose forward!

• **Contact**

The rider is satisfied. He considers his horse to be "relaxed" and "in balance", since it is leaning less on the hand. In fact, its weight is shifted over the shoulders and it is very uncomfortable, only leaning less on the bit because it is behind the hand. Balance and contact therefore become disconnected from each other and from reality.

The horse learns to duck behind the bit to avoid taking a contact. By so doing there is a risk that it also goes "behind the leg" and may even refuse to go forward.

We can say goodbye to balance, and we can also say goodbye to impulsion as well!

To sum up: overbending, an unnatural attitude obtained by hands that are pulled backwards and by various restraining devices, is a vulgar approach to the "mise en main" and arises from a serious lack of knowledge of the horse. That stars of the international dressage scene attempt to justify it and promote it under the name of "rollkur" or "hyperflexion" makes no difference. It is an authoritarian and brutal approach to domination that significantly deprives the horse of its capacities and places "man's noblest conquest" in the position of a slave restrained in shackles.

In terms of locomotion: since the shoulders are weighted and restricted in movement, the horse precipitates the movement of its forelegs in walk. Blocked and compressed instead of stretching and playing its balancing role, the neck does not stretch the back muscles and gradually stifles the natural swinging of the spine (the motor of locomotion): the back no longer functions and the hindquarters trail behind.

Blocked spine, rushing forelegs and lazy hindlegs: this leads to the horse lateralising its walk and almost ambling, a serious gait defect. Very often the horse no longer bascules its back and tends to have a flat canter, like an amble.

In terms of balance: since it overloads its blocked shoulders, the horse gets used to working with the weight shifted onto the forehand.

When it comes to collection, the horse drops its poll instead of growing at the withers and comes under in front - therefore on the shoulders. In addition, the contraction of the back will stop the croup from flexing and the hindquarters engaging. Overall, since the horse cannot rebalance itself on its haunches it will only be able to give a very mediocre shuffle instead of a piaffe.

Historically, all the masters condemned overbending outright. Baucher himself, whose "first manner" could have some of its consequences, went on to correct them with his "second manner" (described by Faverot de Kerbrecht, but unfortunately not very well known).

FEI rules also recommend "... the head slightly in front of the vertical" (ART. 401 - 406). And yet we regularly see horses that are overbent, that amble instead of collecting the walk and that piaffe whilst coming under in front winning and being placed, even at the top level. What is the purpose of a discipline that does not apply its own rules? It makes the fault become standard or worse still, exemplary.

Overbending results in extreme flexing of the front part of the neck and blocking of its base without stretching the ilio-spinal muscles. The back is blocked as can be seen here with the vertical tail and faulty locomotion. Photo: Toffi

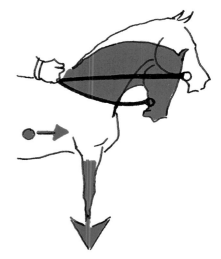

An overbent horse appears to be light. It no longer has contact on the bit. But contrary to what its rider may think, it is neither "relaxed" nor "in balance" and has instead shifted its weight to its shoulders and dropped behind the bit.

So what is the merit of a riding approach which, through its obsession with working the back, often leads to the perverting of a natural gait? What should we think of a system which, through its obsession with engagement of the hindquarters, regularly leads to a piaffe on the forehand and a ridiculous parody of collection?

The stated goal of competitive dressage is:

"Preserving equestrian art from the abuses to which it can be exposed and preserving it in the purity of its principles, so that it can be handed on intact to generations of riders to come." (FEI ART.419)

A very worthy declaration of intent, but when the facts disprove the principles to this extent, we need to look for the deep rooted causes of these very major distortions. This is what we will now do.

When it is correctly understood, overbending is not only an unjustifiable technical option, but it is also purely and simply an abusive treatment and it should therefore be identified as such.
• Judges should mark down competitors presenting horses in this abnormal attitude by at least three points for each figure.
• The rules should eliminate horses that lateralise their walk.
• Imitation piaffes should be unacceptable and scored to ensure that the competitor is not placed.
No discipline can claim to transform each of its competitors into irreproachable riders, but we could at least expect dressage to dissuade incorrect practices and therefore protect the horses that are placed under its jurisdiction. Unfortunately we cannot help but observe that a lack of knowledge of the horse, technical inconsistency and permissiveness have led to modern-day dressage straying a long way from this idea.

Solution:
Extending (telescoping) the neck

Only by extending/telescoping the neck can we stretch and round the top line, at the same time as managing a young horse's natural balance and forwards movement.

Why?

• The anterior insertions of the ilio-spinal muscles advance, which puts these muscles in extension. The dorso-lumbar segment raises and strengthens. The horse forms an arc under the load and carries it better.
• The brachio-cephalic muscles become more horizontal when stretched. They can therefore pull the shoulders a long way forward.
• A horse which has learned to telescope the neck at the same time learns to take the reins in a forwards movement with the noseline always in front of the vertical.
What could be more natural that a telescoped neck allowing for extended/natural gaits!
• An extended neck is more laterally flexible. It will be easier to bend and fully participate in the periodic swinging of the spine that is necessary for well developed gaits. The walk will be preserved and even improved.
• Extending the neck is a decisive factor in forwards movement since it moves the centre of gravity forwards and encourages extended movement as well as getting the horse to take up a contact.

Experience of "rigid reins" (reported by General L'Hotte) on horses that refuse to go forward is very useful in helping people to understand both the dangers of overbending and the virtues of extending the neck with the poll open.

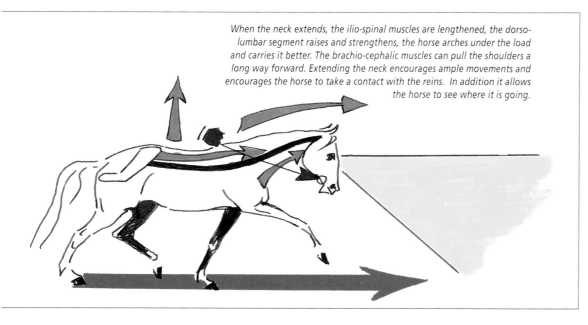

When the neck extends, the ilio-spinal muscles are lengthened, the dorso-lumbar segment raises and strengthens, the horse arches under the load and carries it better. The brachio-cephalic muscles can pull the shoulders a long way forward. Extending the neck encourages ample movements and encourages the horse to take a contact with the reins. In addition it allows the horse to see where it is going.

In fact, pushing the head forwards obliges the horse to move and allows us to restore obedience to the legs on even the most disobedient subjects. A guaranteed result, and without the need to fight.

- Extending the neck is a powerful corrective tool.
  It stretches and relaxes short and tight top lines.
  It strengthens and raises long, weak and loose top lines.
  It reshapes ewe-necks.
  It gives smoother movements to horses that have a sharp knee movement in their foreleg when trotting due to their neck coming out very high at the withers.

How?

What natural way can we use to cause and teach a horse to extend its neck?

A ewe-neck corresponds to a bilateral shortening of the splenius and complexus with stretching of the brachio-cephalic muscles.

If the horse is asked to give a pronounced bend of the neck, the splenius, complexus and brachio-cephalic muscles on the concave side are shortened whilst those on the convex side are lengthened.

Anatomically and mechanically there is incompatibility between a pronounced bending of the neck and either a ewe-neck or an overbent neck.

The whole muscle system in the neck switches from being blocked in the vertical plane to ample movement in the horizontal plane.

If a rider knows how to give a pronounced bend to the neck he will be able to apply lateral suppling exercises to the horse which will quickly give extension of the neck without the use of force because it is done naturally.

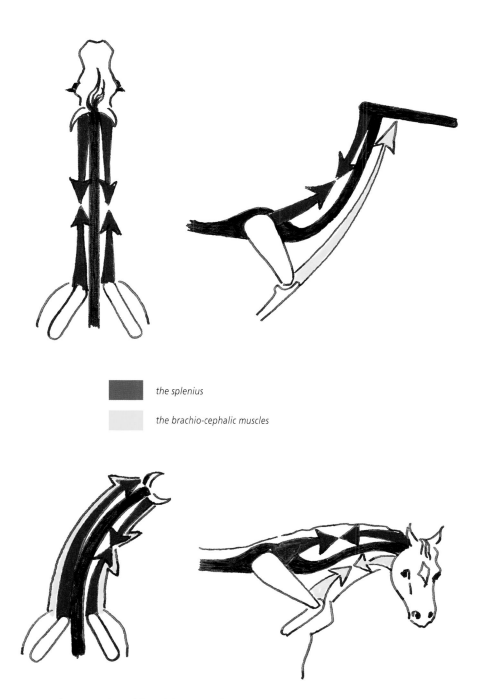

the splenius

the brachio-cephalic muscles

A ewe-neck corresponds to a bilateral shortening of the splenius and complexus with a stretching of the brachio-cephalic muscles. If the horse is asked to give a pronounced bend of the neck, the splenius, complexus and brachio-cephalic muscles on the concave side shorten whereas those on the convex side lengthen. This is why there is incompatibility between a pronounced bending of the neck and both a ewe-neck and an overbent neck.

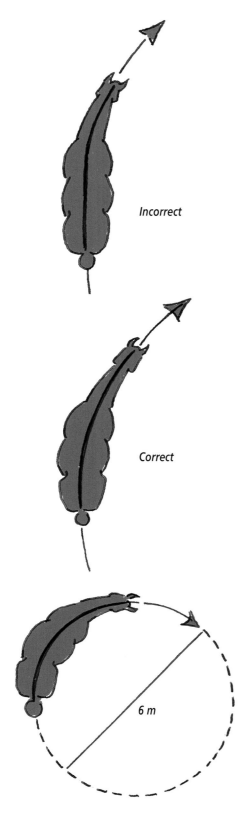

Incorrect

Correct

6 m

Illustrations from dressage manuals show the way that a horse should have an overall bend on the circle according to the official theory. The bending of the neck must remain limited to the same overall bend as the whole spine, perfectly matched to the curve that the horse is on. (Drawings reproduced from B1, pages 108 and 111)

Official theory

This distinguishes between "lateral flexion" and "overall bend":

> *"A horse is said to be 'flexed' when its head is held to one side at the poll... the spine is not involved in this and remains straight."*
> *"The term 'overall bend' is used when a horse is bent throughout its whole longitudinal axis, the whole length of its spine."*
> *"A rider must avoid asking for too much bend of the head and the neck and must focus on correct costal flexion around his inside leg."*
> *"Flexibility must be used to the full in order to increase the suppleness of the horse."*
> *"A six metre circle is called a volte, and is only asked for in collected paces since it requires a high degree of overall bend."*
> *(B1, page 88)*

To sum up: bending of the neck must remain restricted to the anatomical possibilities of the overall bend of the whole spine.

Pronounced overall bend is only possible in collected paces.

This does not take much account of anatomical realities and is certainly not concerned with contradictions!

Anatomy of the spine

• The five sacral vertebrae are welded together and constitute the sacrum. Therefore there is no lateral bending at this level.

• Due to the presence of long transversal apophyses and inter-transversal joints L4-L5, L5-L6 and L6-S1 have no lateral bending.
• As opposed to this L6-S1 gives significant freedom of rotary movement to the sacro-iliac section.
• Between L1 and L4 lateral bending remains very limited.
• The dorsal segment has a very limited capacity for lateral bending between D18 and D14 but this increases between D14 and D9. These vertebrae are connected to the asternal ribs (floating ribs).
From D8 to D1, at the withers, lateral bending is virtually non – existent due to very strong supra-spinal ligaments which connect the long spinal apophyses and the linking of each vertebra to the sternum (sternal ribs).
• The cervical segment is very flexible. At liberty, a horse does not restrict the use of its neck, it uses it and can even bend it 180° to scratch its side.
N.B.: Inter-vertebral lateral bending is always associated with slight rotation.
• In muscular terms the ilio-spinal muscles are inserted on the external faces of the vertebrae at the base of the neck. Therefore, the more the neck is bent the more this favours stretching of the dorsal-lumbar muscle system on the convex side, and shortens it on the concave side.

Therefore, limiting the bending of the neck to the possibilities of the dorso-lumbar segment comes down to virtually not bending it at all since the latter is not very flexible over almost half of its whole length. Under these conditions how can we talk about fully using flexibility?

How can we supple the whole back without using and developing the flexibility of the part of the spine with the most freedom to benefit the others?

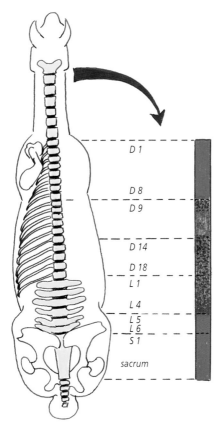

The spine of the horse is only very flexible at the neck. Segments with little lateral-bending capability are shown in blue. Segments with no lateral-bending capability are shown in red.

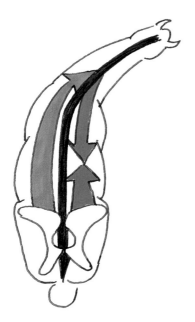

The ilio-spinal muscles are inserted on the external faces of the vertebrae at the base of the neck. Therefore the more the neck is bent, the more the dorsal-lumbar muscle system can stretch on the convex side and shorten on the concave side.

None of this makes sense. As a multi-medal winning rider whose orthodox approach to dressage is beyond suspicion, Harry Boldt published a book called *The dressage Horse* (Haberbeck). It is full of photos taken from above the horse which all show that the horse always bends its neck much more than its back… the latter remains virtually straight, even in lateral work. Compared with the dressage manuals, these photos would be considered incorrect.

> Anatomical facts prove that overall bend of the whole horse is a figment of the imagination.

Overall bending and collection

By definition, collection shortens the horse's body and therefore reduces the margin for lateral flexibility. The shorter a wooden stick, the harder it is to bend.

In collected gaits, the swinging of the spine reduces in the horizontal plane and increases in the vertical plane (the movements gain in terms of elasticity and elevation what they lose in extension). We cannot increase everything at once.

If a collected horse finds it easier to stay on a six metre circle (and why not five and a half metres?), this is not because it is more flexible. On the contrary… it is due to better balance. In fact, it is not by collecting the horse but by extending its neck that the spine has the most amplitude in terms of lateral movement.

A correctly suppled horse can easily stay on a six metre, even a five or a four metre circle without the haunches escaping… by having a pronounced bend of an extended neck. In any case, the back cannot anatomically achieve this degree of bend.

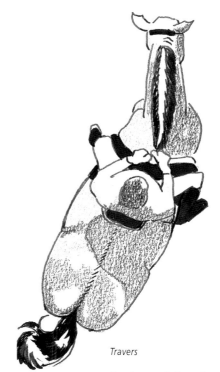

Travers

Drawings made from photos in Das Dressurpferd by Harry Boldt.

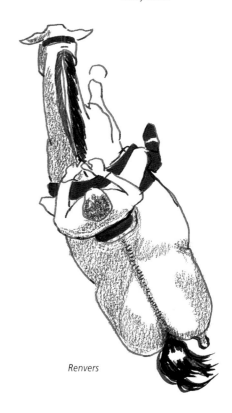

Renvers

Photos taken from above the horse in Das Dressurpferd by Harry Boldt show that all horses always bend their neck a lot more than their back – the latter remaining virtually straight, even in lateral work.

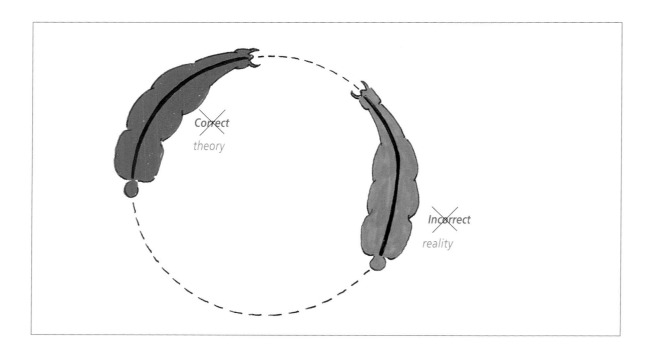

In summary, modern dressage prohibits the pronounced bending of the neck and holds up overall bend as an ideal. Anatomy does not restrict itself to such geometrical demands. These principles are in no way related either to anatomical realities or to common sense since they basically recommend: "Suppling your horse fully but virtually without bending it!" (Here we can find the simplistic concept of straightness.)

These are dogmas - people are asked to learn them and repeat them, naturally without trying to understand them. "Dream of overall bend and suppleness, use training aids and overbending as much as you want, but do not bend the neck!" Riding a horse whilst limiting the bending of its neck to the curve of the figure you are on can be an honourable objective for a presentation, but naturally it is not a rational working method.

Confusing the means and the end to this extent boils down to teaching the following: "To do correct dressage: firstly take an easy and gifted horse... and have him endlessly repeat what the judges want to see in the dressage test". Dancers and gymnasts do not fall prey to this sort of confusion in their training strategies. It is promoting laborious "drilling" to the detriment of a true gymnastic education, and opening the door to all sorts of expedients (see the vast array of training aids and other restrictive devices used in today's riding). Naturally, these simplistic concepts prove inoperable with less gifted or difficult horses that are arbitrarily thrown on the scrap heap.

Many masters have recommended pronounced bending of the neck without becoming lost in the theory of overall bend:

• among them, F. Baucher, whom it is currently fashionable to reject out of hand, preferably without having studied him...
• but also Ludwig Hünersdorf (1748 – 1813) in his *The Most Natural and Easiest Method for Schooling Horses*, 1791:

"After halting, either to rest, or before taking the horse back to the stable, we should be careful to bend the head and neck laterally."
"Normally he will lower his head to the rider's foot in order to make the movement easier."
"The flexibility of the head and neck is so essential that we can see the greatest masters trying to achieve it."

• And above all, La Guérinière, who is willingly referred to by official dressage... without really knowing him:

"Therefore, when we use the right hand rein to bend the horse to the right, we must have the impression that the outside contact remains in the left hand in order for the bend to come from the withers rather than from the end of the nose, which is an incorrect action."

• Parrocel's engravings which illustrate *The School of Horsemanship* show horses that are regularly bent to an angle of 45° in lateral exercises.
• As for Parrocel's preparatory hand-sketched studies of daily work, they show horses with lateral bending of up to 90°! (Published in "François Robichon de La Guérinière, écuyer du roi et d'aujourd'hui", Editions Belin, seminar under the guidance of P. Franchet d'Esperey).

Indeed, La Guérinière and Baucher both reject the use of any training aids... not entirely surprising in view of the above!

Circle to the left. draft: Mähler

Travers to the left. draft: Mähler

Many masters have recommended pronounced bending of the neck, including François Robichon de La Guérinière, Ludwig Hünersdorf, and François Baucher. The two sketches in the top left hand corner show that La Guérinière worked his horses with a lateral bend that could be anything up to 90° (according to two sketches by Parrocel taken from "*François Robichon de La Guérinière, écuyer du roi et d'aujourd'hui* " Editions Belin, seminar under the guidance of P.Franchet d'Esperey.)

The two engravings below are taken from works by Hünersdorf and Baucher.

The pronounced bending of the neck is a fundamental component in the gymnastic training progression...

... which above all allows us to equally stretch and supple the muscles on both sides of the neck.
Photos: Laurioux

33

Conclusion

Dressage must take its principles from studying the horse rather than trying to make the horse fit a mould of preconceived ideas formed into dogmas, which are contrary to nature and forceful.

Trainers in all sports know that careful and useful muscle work must start with stretching sessions. The horse is an athlete and the rider should behave like a skilful trainer. He must be careful not to set the neck and shorten it but must use it to stretch the horse's muscular system... one half at a time using pronounced and repeated lateral bending. This will naturally lead to longitudinal extension (lengthening of the neck) through a gymnastic approach and without any use of force.

> **Principle to remember: longitudinal flexibility results from the development of lateral flexibility.**

Training

Extending of the neck, determined by its lateral flexibility, should be a priority in schooling a young horse or reschooling previously ruined horses.

It should be a key point in warming up any horse, whatever its level.

It should also be used between more difficult work sequences and help bring the horse back to a calm state.

Anyone claiming to educate a horse by using training gadgets is admitting their inability in terms of the mise en main, at the very least.

In the end we can wonder what skills are involved when we anchor the mouth to the girth in order to place a horse's head? The most ignorant of grooms can do this. And what about respecting the mouth?... What

about the all-too frequent and sometimes irreparable accidents?

What is the point of imposing an attitude through an authoritarian system of restraint? Is it not more intelligent in equestrian terms to know and use the horse's nature rather than inventing instruments of restraint?

What would you think about a dance trainer who tied strings to his students in order to set them in a frame? Or a swimming trainer who kept his lifejacket and flippers on when he was working? Are we allowed to tie our opponent's arms behind his back in judo or in boxing in order to get the better of him?

These are all good questions to which the answers are obvious.

Skill resides in more knowledge of the horse and fewer authoritarian palliatives - more equestrian intelligence and less force.

Among the vast array of systems that are available on the market, side reins are the most authoritarian and the most detrimental. They set a single attitude, block all lateral movement of the neck and virtually always end up overbending the horse – everything we should not be doing.

And yet they are used virtually systematically in the dressage world... and are even institutionalised in bastions of "classical" dressage claiming to be descendents of La Guérinière. His *School of Horsemanship* does not even mention them!

"Off-the-shelf" solutions, although very appealing, are very unlikely to improve training.

Teaching

To teach the basics: an independent seat and the elementary school of aids... a teacher needs to make up for the student's inability to round the horse himself. This is important in order to preserve the horse and ensure the student's comfort and the quality of the lesson.

A training aid for teaching novice riders according to Phillipe Karl: in order to teach basics to a novice rider, an instructor will use a "variable geometry" type of training aid. An example of this is "draw reins" that are free to run in a ring that is connected to the pommel of the saddle. Initially the reins will be connected to side rings on the cavesson (a gogue may also be suitable).

This is therefore THE unique situation in which it is important to use a training aid as the lesser of two evils, for a good cause! The device should be of "variable geometry", leaving the horse free to bend its neck and be adjusted sufficiently long so as not to overbend him.

For example "draw reins" that are free to slide through a ring connected to the pommel of the saddle and that therefore allow the horse to bend, would be perfect for this purpose. Firstly on the lunge and then without the lunge, the student will learn the different rein effects to allow him to use the neck in a rational manner.

To protect the horse from faults that the student will naturally commit when he is learning, the instructor will use the following progression:

• reins connected to the side rings of a cavesson
• reins connected to the bit rings

The training aid will only be removed when the student has proven that he has sufficient control over his hands.

In this way students learn to respect the horse's mouth and the instructor preserves his mounts.

Presentation of novice horse classes

Presenting young horses in a spectacular extended trot with the rider sitting the trot, is one of the rituals of the dressage world.

With high neck carriage due to good conformation, the horse is unable to stretch its back muscles and is pushed into impressive extensions through naturally flattering locomotion, the horse contracts its back. It "flings" its legs out much more in front than it pushes behind, just like the crawl in swimming.

This is an abuse of the horse's natural aptitudes: a sort of exhibitionism that is paid for by the horse.

It is like revving your Ferrari's engine by driving 100 miles per hour in second gear, before running it in – a good way of breaking it quickly.

Extended trot should not be included in the programme of horses that are not yet advanced in their collected work and should be banned from presentations of young horses.

Young horses should only be presented in a "lengthened" trot with the neck stretched and with the rider in rising trot.

Followed in this way, the rules would oblige riders to work on extending the neck instead of using tricks and to respect the horse's back instead of crushing it whilst holding in the head – with the excuse of having a correct dressage seat.

In this way we would leave a small chance to horses that are less gifted but that have been worked correctly, and we would avoid compromising the future of the best ones.

> **The more breeding progresses, the more there is a need for serious safeguards. Too many marvellous horses are victims of their talent and generosity through absurd fashions.**

NO

YES

Young horses should not be presented in a spectacular extended trot in which they strongly contract their back. They should only show a "lengthened trot" with an extended neck and with the rider in rising trot.

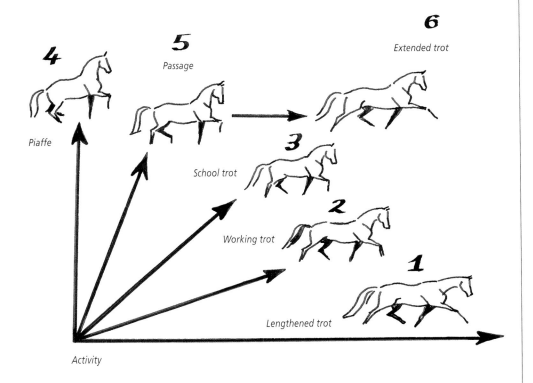

The gymnastic progression in dressage should lead from the lengthened trot to the working trot then to the school trot, to the piaffe and to the passage and finish with the extended trot.

THE HAND

According to the dressage manuals the hands must act with the active support of the propulsive aids. The hand must be held low and aligned with the elbow and the mouth.

"The aim of Art is not only to ride a well conformed animal, but to get the very best out of those that have been less gifted by nature..."
(Ludwig Hünersdorf, 1748–1813)

The dressage manuals say nothing about horses with difficult conformation.

Using the hand

Summary of principles governing the use of the hand:
• Holding the reins: all fingers closed on the reins, the thumb closed lightly.
• Position: hold the hand low and aligned with the elbow and the mouth.
• Rein effects: the hand can release, resist or request, but in any case, the reins must only be used with the active support of the "propulsive aids" (seat and legs).

Firstly, we can note that the illustrations in dressage manuals always show horses with perfect conformation that are already flexed at the poll, with their head on the vertical.

Necks with less good or frankly poor conformation are nowhere to be seen. We can read two things into this:

• either this means that horses with difficult conformation are not worth training- which is difficult to believe
• or it means that the current system does not have an opinion on a subject which poses it some problems- and yet difficult situations are when a method can best prove its worth.

So, not only is this fundamental and tricky question of how to school a horse to the hand considered from the most advantageous angle, but the problem is also considered to be solved in advance. If someone gave in an essay like this, the teacher would mark it with the following: "misses the point".

Holding the reins and position of the hand

When riding an unschooled horse (therefore one in a natural attitude), a rider holding the reins with all of his fingers closed and fixed low hands will immediately cause the horse to resist.

Held in this way, the hand opposes the mouth with a fixed point and imposes a very harsh contact on it.

How much lightness can we have in the fingers with a fist closed on the reins? None. You can play a bass drum or a bugle wearing boxing gloves, but not a guitar or a piano.

This results in the horse desperately trying to come over the bit, setting up a confrontational situation from the outset.

The resisting hand

"A resisting rein is used when the horse goes against or above the contact."
"To use this aid, the hands close strongly without changing their position, until the horse yields to the bit and becomes light in the hand."
"This aid must be combined with a supporting back and pushing legs."
(B1, page 66)

It is easy to see why such authoritarian use of the hand needs to be combined with support from propulsive aids: we have to compensate for the retroactive effect of a hand that opposes the forwards movement.

In addition, this opposition will contradict and dull the horse's obedience to the legs. "Release the brakes on a bike and you won't have to peddle so hard... and for nothing!"

Since this "bike" is also a living and sensitive being, which above all needs to understand us, we can question the educational value of such contradictions.

In general, the harder the rider pushes the horse towards a resisting hand, the more a horse will fight. This will start a vicious circle which sometimes leads to the horse leaping forwards, rearing or refusing to go forward at all.

But the manual has a solution:

> *"With this fault, the horse's head opens way in front of the vertical. The horse does not want to flex its poll and uses the under-neck muscles to resist the hand."*
> *"...lungeing the horse with side reins can be very beneficial. The side reins must be quite short to start with."*
> (B1, page 145)

Besides the fact that the horse goes over the bit by contracting the top muscles in its neck rather than the lower ones (anatomical logic), this approach is primitively coercive: "You don't want to lower your nose? Then I'll tie your mouth to the girth, and nice and short to start with!"

When things go badly, the horse will be panic stricken, painfully trapped and may put up a violent fight, sometimes to the point of being irreparably ruined (horses that rear up and fall backwards).

When things go "well", to avoid the crushing pressure on its tongue, the horse will simply drop behind the bit.

The horse's attitude has been imposed by a very primitive means of restraint, but the rider is satisfied – he will be able to ride it with his fists planted firmly on each side of the horse's withers, and the horse will abundantly flex its poll- and probably overbend in the process.

The active hand

It is recommended to start by closing the fingers, but this is naturally impossible since we already have "closed fingers" to hold the reins. In fact, with low hands and closed fingers on the reins, the rider can only really act by moving his hand backwards, or in other words by pulling.

This is the rather unpleasant reality hidden behind the discreet expression "active rein": a hypocritical way of not saying "pull on the reins" whilst knowing full well that the rider can do nothing else.

Whether to control the speed and balance using the "demi-arrêt", or to bend using a "regulating" outside rein, the manual goes on:

> *"For this aid, as for the others, the hand must remain low."*

This leads to riders who tend to pull left and right to get the horse to yield, or on both reins to slow down, stop and rein-back, naturally while still applying the propulsive aids.

Some may pull with more skill than others. We could almost say they have a "good hand". However their endorsement cannot justify the method.

Since it gets into the habit of flexing at the poll to escape the pain inflicted by the hands which it encounters every time it lifts its nose, the horse will respond to the rider's action on one rein by flexing more at the poll instead of bending its neck (especially on the convex side, of course).

That this system is not conducive to lateral flexions of the neck and indulgent towards overbending is not really surprising – it is the logical consequence of the retroactive use of the hand and a coercive conception of submission.

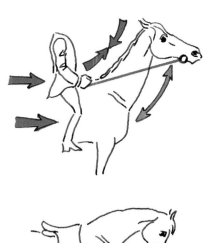

For a horse that goes above the bit, the dressage manuals recommend that the rider pushes on a low resisting hand and that he lunges the horse with side reins that are initially adjusted quite short. In reality the horse reacts by dropping behind the bit to avoid its tongue being crushed.

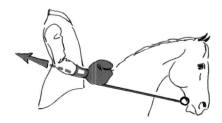

Since he has to keep his hands low and his fingers closed on the reins, the rider can only act by pulling back.

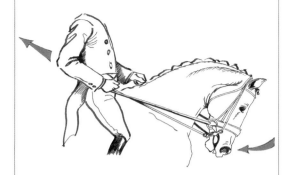

To escape from the pain caused by the rider's hands, the horse tends to respond to the tension in one single rein by closing its poll angle more than it bends its neck: it overbends

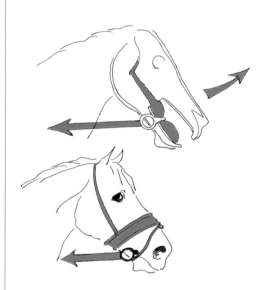

The lower the hand is held, the harder it acts on the tongue, a hypersensitive organ. Specially designed nosebands to stifle the horse's protests are the rule today.

Mouth problems

Whether "resisting" or "active", the lower the hand, the more its effects are focused on the tongue. However, this is a highly vascularised organ, full of nerves and covered in mucus tissues, and therefore hypersensitive. To protect its tongue from the discomfort inflicted by the hand, the horse may possibly try to pull it back in its mouth, stick it out to the side, put it over the bit, etc.

Solution: specially designed crank nosebands that can be shut tightly. They can either be single or double, and a triple version is certainly just around the corner!

Their sole purpose is to stifle the horse's protests and hide the perverse effects of a hand that is harsh on the mouth: a constraining approach using instruments of restraint, once again!

This is quite a strange dialogue between two people, one asking impolitely and the other who has been gagged!

These devices have become standardised and generalised because today's dressage has no other solution to the detrimental consequences of its stated principles. Humans are naturally very indulgent when it comes to their own problems.

It is certainly more satisfying for a rider to accuse a horse of having a "bad mouth", rather than challenging their own equestrian concepts, and even easier to change the bit, the noseband or the training aid rather than changing their hand…

All that remains to escape the pain is for the horse to overbend and grind its teeth in protest (and to mask this, it is common to apply various products to the teeth just before tightening the noseband).

Conclusion

All-in-all this approach to using the hand is easily summed up: keep you hands low in all circumstances and flex the poll by whatever means it takes.

The rider starts by forcing poll flexion using instruments of restraint (side reins, draw reins, etc.) in contempt of a mouth that is condemned to silence (special nosebands).

He then uses all his skill to reproduce and prolong the effects of these palliative measures with low hands – using draw reins for back-up if necessary.

Pulling in this way requires the constant use of propulsive aids to compensate and encourages overbending.

The disastrous consequences of one obsession: low hands. The systematic use of instruments of restraint results from a coercive approach which itself results from a concept of the use of the hand that is contrary to nature.

The same is true in many circumstances: mistaken principles naturally lead to authoritarian methods and rough processes.

Why not look at the question from a more general point of view: imagine parents who consult a child psychiatrist because they have a young and very turbulent child.

How would you judge a specialist educator who recommends that the child be gagged and tied to his chair, without even asking about the educational principles of the parents?

Under such conditions we can see why dressage manuals only focus on well conformed horses that are already submissive to the hand: in fact they are much more focused on the "dressage" use of previously conditioned, gifted subjects rather than schooling itself. In this respect a dressage manual should explain how to educate an unschooled horse to the hand even if it has previously been ruined, whether or not it has good conformation and without the use of devices- a completely different story!

Without this there can be no respect for the horse, real riding skills or credibility of the instructor.

And yet side reins or draw reins and crank nosebands have become the accepted norm, and low hands with clenched fingers on constantly tight reins have become institutionalised. And a student will not be welcome to ask for any explanation that is worthy of its name, for the simple reason that it is impossible to justify.

> Prejudices held up as principles lead to teaching with poor content, presented in an authoritarian manner. This is a real shame since teaching, just like schooling horses, above all involves improving understanding.

Issues involved in the mise en main

What difficulties are involved in educating the horse to the hand (the mise en main – see glossary)? These can be summed up in two points:

> *Resistance to bending: "On the left side the neck muscles are stiff and resistant. We call this the stiff side. However the difficult side is the hollow side, the right side." (B1, page 147.)*
> *Resistance in the poll: "Against the hand, above the bit."In this fault, the horse's nose is well in front of the vertical. The horse does not want to flex the poll and uses the under-neck muscles resist to the hand."*
> *(FN Guidelines for Riding and Driving German Equestrian Federation, vol. 1, page 145.)*

Stiffness to the left

Experiment: take a horse that is considered totally "stiff" to the left. Place yourself next to its left shoulder and take a carrot out of your pocket. It will come and take it and bend around you at an angle of 90° without any difficulty. Any horse bends its neck 180° to scratch its hindquarters!

The theory of muscular "stiffness" to the left is therefore not valid. It is false in two respects:

If there was stiffness this would be to the right and not to the left. The rider feels a resistance in his left hand, but it is the muscles on the right of the neck which are contracted and oppose the lateral flexion.

"Stiffness" would mean: physical impossibility of bending. However, we have seen that this is not the case.

There is no inability, but there is refusal. This is therefore not stiffness but a contraction, naturally caused by the action on the mouth since, with one hand placed on the horse's head you would easily be able to move the head to one side.

Resisting more by contraction than natural stiffness, the horse is more in need of relaxing than suppling.

Above all, the hand must relax the horse in order to then bend it and therefore help to supple it.

Focusing on "gymnasticising, suppling and muscling" is thinking like a bodybuilder rather than a rider, since riding basically involves relaxing and balancing.

Naturally a horse that works in tension gradually loses its original suppleness over the years. This will end up damaging its physical health and even shortening its life.

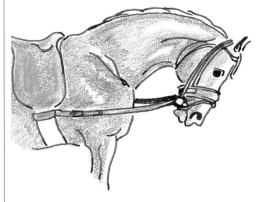

A rider who forces flexion of the poll with training aids and shuts the mouth with special nosebands is really no better than a teacher who gags a child and ties him to his chair to silence him and make him calm.

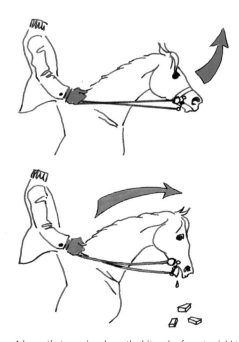

All horses can bend the neck to the left to take a treat. A horse that refuses to bend the neck under saddle therefore does not act due to stiffness but due to contraction of the right side of the neck caused by the painful action of the rider's left hand.

A horse that remains above the bit and refuses to yield to hands that are fixed on each side of the withers will round its neck itself when mobilising its jaw and tongue to eat a sugar lump.

Is the poll the seat of resistance?

To start with, remember that the horse goes above the hand by contracting the muscles on the top of its neck rather than those underneath. The manual has definitely got a problem with anatomy.

Experiment: take a horse that has resisted all possible efforts and remained above the hand, with a stiff poll and neck. Sit on it and at halt try to get it to yield by fixing your hands, one each side of the withers, as hard as you can. Result: nothing happens. Keep your hands in this "regulatory" position. Then ask an assistant to come and undo the "regulatory" noseband and to give the horse a few sugar lumps. To take them the horse will unlock its jaw, and to crunch and swallow them it will move its tongue and salivate.

While doing this it will also play with its bit and then round its poll itself... at the same time giving you the exquisite feeling of a mouth that is alive and friendly and that moulds perfectly to your hand.

This is a horse with a "gallant mouth" as described by La Guérinière and a "display of lightness" resulting from a "cession de machoire" (release of the jaw – see glossary) as described by Baucher. In any case, it definitely means that the seat of the "problems" is not in the poll but in the relationship between the hand and the mouth once again!

Conclusion

When the bit acts strongly on the tongue, a hypersensitive organ, the horse apprehends the hand like you fear pain at the dentist.

Extending the metaphor: if the clumsy dentist pinches your tongue with his forceps... you will jump in the dentist's chair straining your body, with your neck arching backwards.

If in addition, instead of apologising he says: "You've got problems in your neck!" you will accuse him of incompetency and insincerity.

All that is left for this fraud is to gag you so that he no longer hears your protests! One thing is certain: you will change your dentist.

Therefore saying that the horse's problems are in the poll is simply mistaking the effects for the cause – once again.

In the same way, we could also conclude that "resistance to the leg is basically found in the tail" because a horse swishes its tail in response to the use of spurs.
Ridiculous, don't you agree?

> Not only are theories on the "stiffness of the neck" and the "problem poll" totally mistaken but they also incriminate the horse instead of placing the responsibility on the rider: a rather underhand way of thinking about the horse, which also legitimises the rider's authoritarian approach.

Explanations

The tongue, the pharynx and the larynx are attached to an osteo-cartilaginous part of the body called the hyoid bone, situated between the branches of the lower jawbone.

Mobilising the tongue depends on muscles that link the hyoid bone to the sternum (sterno-hyoidian), to the head (occipital bone) and the shoulders (scapular aponeurosis).

The hyoid bone and the tongue are therefore a crossroads of the whole forehand... nothing happens that does not pass through here.

Resistant low hands? These mistreat the tongue and cause blockage of the hyoid bone with generalised contraction of the jaw, the poll, the neck and the shoulders.

The more the rider resists, the more the horse feels pain, the more it contracts and the more the rider – must resist a vicious circle. This is even truer since the prolonged pressure of the bit has a tourniquet effect on the tongue: the blood finds it increasingly difficult to circulate; the tongue becomes dry, sometimes blue, and increasingly insensitive.

The "SUGAR LUMP effect": as opposed to this, a sugar lump causes the lower jaw and tongue to mobilise. This frees the hyoid bone and consequently relaxes the poll, the neck and the shoulders. Since it is relaxed, the forehand becomes flexible again and the horse no longer has any reason, nor any way, to fight against the hand.

"Relaxing the mouth basically involves a movement of the tongue similar to that it makes when swallowing." (General Decarpentry, Academic Equitation)

If the rider has a clever enough hand to cause this mobilising of the jaw and the tongue, he will trigger behaviour that is similar to swallowing, with production of saliva… and this time without the sugar lump.

By causing the jaw to release, the rider will be able to re-establish overall relaxation of the horse when he wants. In addition, he will instantly stop or eliminate many of the visible effects of rejection:

• As long as the horse is in a cession de mâchoire, it does not hold its tongue up and does not put it over the bit.
• As long as it mobilises its jaw it cannot grind its teeth.

As long as the horse releases its jaw and is in a cession de mâchoire, the rider will be guaranteed its attention, relaxation and bal-ance. As opposed to this, the slightest disturbance will set the mouth and immediately alert the rider.

"Whatever conformation fault in the horse opposes the correct distribution of forces, it is always in the jaw that we can feel the most immediate effect. And since the neck is intimately linked to the jaw, the stiffness of one is immediately communicated to the other."

"If the soft mobility of the jaw continues at every gait, the horse's movement will be dependable, precise and gracious." (Baucher)

Conclusion

There is quite a good metaphor to summerise what we have just looked at (already used by Dominique Olivier):

The head and neck are the "door" through which we take possession of the horse's "house". The mouth is the fragile "lock" to this "door"… and the "cession de machoire" is the "key" itself.

You only need your legs if you want to break down the door – in which case you cannot expect to be made welcome.

In any case, forget the crowbar and blowtorch… you don't break and enter into a friend's house!

Limiting the concept of mise en main to flexing the poll is mistaking the end result for the means. By not having the "key" to the problem, we are forced to solve the problem by force with tools: various training aids, crank nosebands, etc.

Overbending and blocked mouths occur when we break down the "door" and smash

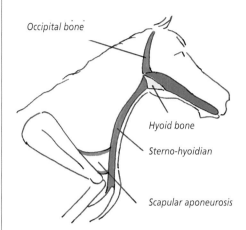

The hyoid bone and the tongue form a crossroads for everything to do with the forehand: the tongue, the pharynx and the larynx are attached to the hyoid bone located between the branches of the lower jawbone. The muscles linking the hyoid bone to the sternum, to the head and to the shoulders determine the mobilisation of the tongue.

A low hand acts backwards, abuses the tongue and causes generalised contraction of the jaw, the poll, the neck and the shoulders. Photo: Toffi

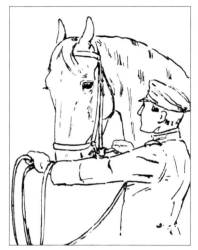

From 1912 to 1926 the Manual of Instruction for the German Cavalry included a series of exercises to mobilise the jaw and to flex the neck.

the "lock" – because a horse stretches into its reins by opening its poll and shows relaxation by mobilising its tongue and its lower jaw.

In a well-thought-out approach to dressage that respects the horse, study of the mise en main must start by the cession de machoire: this is a courteous preliminary that relaxes the horse and from which everything else will naturally result. Making flexing of the poll a priority forces the head's position and approaches the problem from the wrong way.

A little history

The importance of getting the jaw to release prior to any search for the positioning of the head was underlined by many authors, including some of the most famous.

Xenophon (400 BC)
He recommended suppling the neck by relaxing the mouth ("Peri Hippikes", Chapter X).

François Baucher (1796–1873)
He showed students his arm held out straight with his hand in a fist: "I want the strongest of you to try and make me bend my arm"… and I want the weakest of you to tickle me and make me open my fist, to see how they can easily bend my arm".
"The horse will have completely yielded to the action of the hand when its jaw is mobile."

François Faverot de Kerbrech (1837–1905)
"Firstly achieve lightness with the horse's head raised. Flexing of the poll comes later through the softness of the jaw. But the jaw must always release first…"

Alexis L'Hotte (1825–1904)
"Flexing of the poll is not only about the position of the head, it resides above all in the submission of the jaw, which is the first spring that receives the action of the hand. If this spring yields softly to the action that asks it to move, it will lead to the flexibility of the neck and will cause the softness of all the other springs."

Jules Pellier (1800–1874)
"We repeat that a mechanical aid cannot overcome the bad habits taken by an animal and only a knowledgeable and intelligent hand will give the horse mobility of the jaw and the correct position of the head."

James Fillis (1834–1913)
"A horse worked through its mouth can be kept on the hand with a light contact at the end of your fingers whereas another, worked through the poll, requires that the reins and the arms remain tight. This is why the first type of riding is all about a delicate approach and the second is all about force."

NB:
From 1912 to 1926 the *Manual of Instruction for the German Cavalry* included a series of exercises to mobilise the jaw and to flex the neck.

Our current knowledge confirms the sound basis of these principles: osteopaths correct displaced cervical vertebrae and blockages in the poll by opening the mouth and carrying out pronounced lateral flexions of the neck.

Ethologists have highlighted the major role of the mouth in the expressiveness and communication of the horse, in particular concerning submissive behaviour. Monty Roberts calls it "licking". Mobility of the jaw and the tongue: signs of submission and a factor of relaxation! Something that we can use for a friendly and natural control.

Lastly, up until 1958, FEI Rules for dressage included an article stating:

> *"At all paces, slight mobility of the jaw, without nervousness, is the guarantee of submission and the harmonious distribution of forces."*

Subsequently, this important article disappeared without any explanation.

Single or double reinforced nosebands are now the rule, and it is forbidden to present a horse without a noseband.

Worse still, tack judges are not authorised to inspect bits before the rider goes into the arena, as they were in the past: the riders claimed that this operation disturbed their horses.

The most precious equestrian principles, taken from the experience and intuition of the finest masters, and then validated by scientific modern studies, have caved in to the pressure of the professional sector and its interests. This is a serious cultural regression.

Alternative

Aa an approach to achieve the "mise en main", we can list the principles we have already established and look back at their sequence:

• Extension of the neck is the first stage in a rational gymnastic approach to working the horse.
• This is naturally obtained by pronounced lateral flexion which stretches the convex side and starts to round the poll.
• This lateral flexion requires the horse to be permeable to the hand through relaxation.
• Relaxation is guaranteed by "cession de machoire". This is characterised by the mobility of the tongue and of the lower jawbone. The horse lets the bit hang in its mouth and salivates: swallowing behaviour.
• In order to act effectively, whilst respecting the mouth, the hand must not act on the tongue.

The solution to these requirements is obvious.

The only alternative to low hands: raising the hand.

In teaching the horse the rein effects, starting by the action on the corners of the mouth – use a snaffle, upwards.

Movement of the bit towards the gullet causes the jaw to relax, then as soon as the hand is lowered the tongue is mobilised and saliva is produced: swallowing behaviour.

A high position of the head is most favourable to cession de machoire because:

• weight is shifted from the shoulders and the horse cannot lean on the hand
• the sterno-hyoidian bone approaches the vertical and stretches… which facilitates relaxation and mobilisation of the tongue.

On this basis, we can see how best to proceed according to different types of horses.

When the rider pulls on the reins, the horse says "yes" with its head (nods) and "no" in its mind.

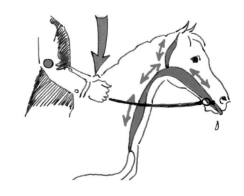

If the rider acts by raising his hands to mobilise the horse's jaw and tongue, and then lowers his hands to leave the bit to hang freely in the mouth, the horse will really say "yes".

Initiation In-hand

For Horses with no specific difficulties (in a snaffle bridle), rather than arbitrarily imposing any specific position on a horse using authoritarian training aids that are detrimental to its mouth, it is much more friendly, efficient and rational to initiate the horse to the main effects of the hand from the ground.

Methodical use of flexions, in-hand and then in the saddle, at halt and then at walk, at trot and lastly at canter, are simply a smart learning approach and good teaching sense.

There is no doubt that we owe this method to François Baucher. Both he and his followers developed a large variety of flexions using both the simple snaffle and the double bridle. This subject alone could fill a whole book.

Without looking at any excessive approaches, we will focus on a well-thought-out selection of the most simple and effective flexions.

Cession de mâchoire

At halt, with the horse straight and on the track, the rider level with the head:

• Adjust the outside rein, passing it over the neck, with the hand near the cheek.
• Take the inside rein and place the index finger in the ring of the snaffle.
• Gradually bring the two hands closer together (in this way the snaffle bit only acts on the corners of the mouth) until the horse distinctly opens its mouth. Release. Very light contact as long as the mouth remains mobile. Start again as soon as the mouth becomes dead. Reward whenever the horse yields.
• Walk a few strides, ask for the jaw to release again, put the horse forward again, etc. until the jaw releases at walk.

Initial cession de mâchoire in-hand: the outside rein is passed over the neck.

The rider takes the inside rein, putting his index finger in the snaffle ring. He gradually brings his two hands closer together until the horse distinctly yields its jaw, then releases his hands and keeps a very light contact as long as the jaw remains mobile. Photos: Laurioux

By repetition, the rider sets up a behaviour pattern that will become a reflex anticipation effect: the horse will yield its mouth increasingly quickly and will tend to keep the released mouth for longer with more and more subtle actions of the hand.

A true dialogue is set up between the hand and the mouth.

Lateral neck flexion

When the horse easily gives its mouth, which can take from a few minutes to a few lessons:

• Start by placing yourself on the outside.
• Take a contact on the inside rein and pass it over the middle of the neck.

Lateral flexion of the neck in-hand: the rider starts by placing himself on the outside: the inside rein passes over the middle of the neck.

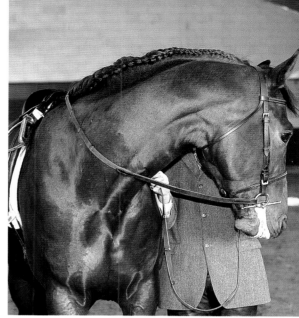

Following this, the rider then stands on the inside. The outside rein passes over the base of the neck. The rider asks for the jaw to release and the lateral flexion by raising the inside snaffle ring towards the poll.

The rider pushes the horse's head in the bend with the outside hand. Photos: Laurioux

N.B.: letting the horse close its poll angle before maintaining a full bend in the neck is similar to teaching it how to get out of the lateral flexion, refusing to take a contact in the outside rein and overbending in the end.

It is therefore a good idea to correctly separate the points in the progression:

1   Cession de mâchoire
2   Full lateral flexion without closing the poll angle
3   Poll flexion without lowering the head
4   Extending the neck

If the horse tries to anticipate and force the hand downwards, oppose this movement using half halts: upward actions with a proportionate amount of strength.

Validate the lateral flexion by getting the jaw to release and maintain the position for a few seconds. Release the reins and reward. If the flexion is successful, the horse maintains its attitude for a few moments and gradually straightens afterwards.

Now, holding the outside ring, push the horse's head to give the required bend. Check the position by getting the jaw to release.

• Repeat this lateral flexion, this time standing on the inside. Take a contact on the outside rein and pass it over the base of the neck, the hand near the middle of the shoulder.

Ask for the jaw to yield by raising the inside snaffle ring towards the poll. Increase the supporting hand until gradually obtaining a bend of 45 or even 90° (for gymnastics purposes) without flexing the poll. The horse therefore learns to softly take a contact in the outside rein (light contact on the tongue initially).

Flexion of the poll and extension of the neck in-hand: the rider firstly asks for the jaw to release in a high position...

... bending the neck...

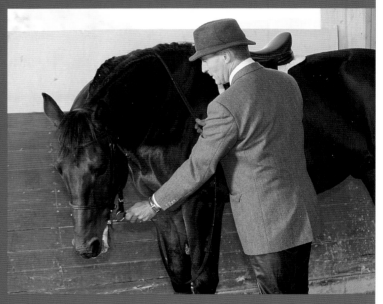

... and causing flexion of the poll whilst resisting on the outside rein. Then releasing...

... and accompanying the horse's mouth down and out.

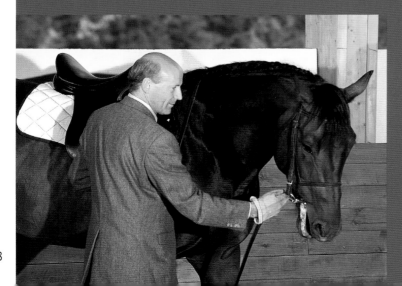

The horse learns to maintain the extension of the neck for increasing amounts of time on both reins and in movement.
Photos: Laurioux

Poll flexion and neck extension

The horse always tries to make it easier to have a pronounced bend by lowering its head.

Ask for a poll flexion by resisting on the outside rein, and release by accompanying the mouth down and out. Maintain the position for a few moments with a released jaw. If the horse tries to overbend or lean on the hands, act using half halts.

Prolong the extending of the neck at walk, on circles, then on straight lines.

Every time the horse tries to come above the hand, raise the inside hand and increase the bend whilst controlling with the outside rein until an extension is obtained once again.

Work under saddle

This involves carefully reproducing the process carried out in-hand. Adjust the reins and hold them between the thumb and bent index finger. The other fingers remain half open so as to be able to play freely on the reins.

Cession de mâchoire

• Place the hands at an appropriate height to align them with your elbows and the mouth.
• Gradually close the fingers whilst slightly turning the wrists (like you turn a door handle) which puts your elbows to the side of your body and avoids the arm moving back, then lift the hands.
• The more the rider lifts his hands, the more he takes a contact on the rein, but this gradual tension is applied to the corners of the mouth… and not at all to the tongue.
• The raising of the snaffle in the mouth causes the jaw to release. Open the fingers and lower the hand. Return to the original position, the hand has a light contact with the tongue, as long as the horse releases its bit.
• Start again as soon as the mouth appears to be dead. Reward often.

Cession de machoire in the saddle: the rider gradually closes his fingers whilst turning his wrists slightly, then he raises his hands.

The horse responds to the raising of the snaffle by releasing its jaw, the rider opens his fingers and lowers his hands.

In this position, the rider's hands hold a light contact to the horse's tongue, while the horse tastes its jaws.
Photos: Laurioux

Lateral flexion of the neck and poll flexion in the saddle.

By gradually lifting the inside hand, the rider asks for the jaw to release then a neck flexion.

He then asks for the poll flexion by resisting on the outside rein and then releasing by lowering and moving his hands forwards.

"Ask often, be content with little, reward generously."
(Étienne Beudant) Photos: Laurioux

Please note: Extending the neck in a pronounced bend corresponds to maximum stretching of the muscles in the outside half of the neck.

Lateral neck flexion

• By slowly raising only the inside hand, get the jaw to release, and then the flexion of the neck.

• Sharp upwards action on both reins (half halt) if the horse tries to force the hand downwards.

• Maintain the lateral flexion for a few seconds without closing the poll and with a released mouth with a light contact on the reins.

The horse then learns to maintain the given position as long as it is not asked to change.

Poll flexion and neck extension

• From a pronounced bend in the neck, ask for a poll flexion by resisting on the outside rein and releasing by lowering and moving the hands forwards.

• Maintain the required position as long as the horse keeps a contact on the reins and has a mobile mouth.

• Half halt every time the horse leans or tries to overbend.

• The neck extension is obtained step-by-step at halt, at walk, at trot and at canter – on circles then on a straight line.

• Gradually the pronounced lateral flexions will no longer be necessary to achieve the neck extension – even though they will remain part of the daily gymnastics routine.

Horses which go above the bit

These horses have an inverted neck, often thin and rising low out of the shoulders ... but they can also have more flattering necks that rise out of the shoulders vertically.

In both cases these horses often totally refuse to take a contact on the reins.

In-hand

• Firstly ask the jaw to release under the usual conditions. First concession.
• Then prolong the tension in the reins beyond the point where the mouth opens and firmly and calmly increase this until the horse lowers the neck and moves the nose forward ever so slightly... which it will always do due to the principle of action-reaction. Release, reward generously and start again.
• The horse very quickly understands that to free himself from this tension, that is not painful but which annoys it, there is only one thing to do: move the hand down and forwards.
• This work, which is started at halt, will then be confirmed at walk.

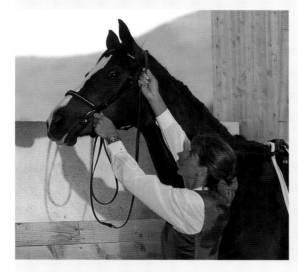

For horses with a ewe-neck, firstly ask for the jaw to release in-hand in a high position.

Prolong the tension in the reins beyond the point where the mouth opens until the horse lowers its nose and moves it ever so slightly forwards.

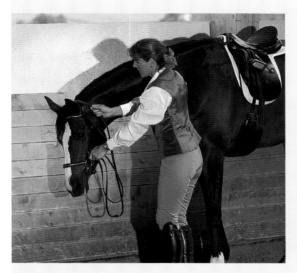

The horse very quickly understands that the only way out of this painless but annoying tension...

... involves taking the head down and out. Photos: Laurioux

> **Please note: The more the horse stretches the more the rider lessens the tension in the reins... without ever breaking the contact.**

With a horse with a ewe-neck, firmly take a contact in both reins and place the hands distinctly higher than the mouth. Increase this tension until the horse tries to lower and move its head forward.

Accompany this movement by lowering the hands and advancing them in the direction of the horse's mouth without breaking the contact.

Turn the wrists and hold them up ...

... then release whilst keeping the contact. Photos: Laurioux

Under saddle

The rider must take a firm contact on both reins, carrying his hands distinctly higher than the mouth so as to only act on the corners of the mouth, prolonging this tension beyond the point where the jaw releases and until the horse tries to lower its head and move it forward. The hand must accompany this movement by becoming softer but without breaking the contact.

The hands will therefore have to follow the head wherever it moves and not become fixed and low until the horse fixes its head with a contact by extending the neck.

The rider's legs will only be involved if the horse is not sufficiently forward.

The horse will be worked with an extended neck until its shape is remodelled. When the base of its neck is stronger and stable, the rider will look for more supporting attitudes, continuing to extend the neck whenever required.

A horse which leans on the hand must firstly learn to carry its neck itself without leaning on the hand from the ground.

Horses which lean on the hand

This is generally the case of horses with very stocky necks that are short and carried low, but any horse with good conformation that encounters rather unsophisticated hands can behave in the same way.

The horse must learn or relearn to hold its neck itself and no longer try to lean on the hand. Anatomy and balance are harder to ignore than any of the latest fashionable dogmas: whether we like it or not, it is by lifting the neck that we lighten the shoulders and the contact. In other words, by teaching a true demi-arrêt (half-halt -see glossary), one that is carried out by acting upwards – and not one that involves pulling with the hands and pushing with the legs at the same time on the pretext of keeping your hands low.

In-hand

• Place yourself in front of the horse at halt, with the horse straight and on the track.
• Place a thumb in each ring of the snaffle and push in the direction of the horse's ears as firmly as necessary to distinctly lift the neck. Maintain a light contact as long as the horse does not try to lean.

• Ask for the jaw to release (gentle pressure on the corners of the mouth) and apply a demi-arrêt (lively and repeated pushing movement) at the slightest leaning on the hand.
• Get the horse to walk by pulling the head towards you, stop it by lifting the neck… and work through to rein-back in the same way. The horse will learn to use its neck to balance and not to fight against the hand. After which the normal sequence of flexions can be considered: lateral flexions and extension of the neck.

Under saddle

• Gently adjust the reins. As soon as the horse starts to lean, turn the wrists and sharply lift them. The surprise effect, that is painless since it is applied to the corners of the mouth, causes the horse to lift its neck. Lower the hand: the hands come back to their basic position, light contact on the reins.
• This will be repeated until the horse releases its jaw, keeping a high head carriage and without trying to lean on the hands – at halt, at walk, at a small trot and even at canter.

As soon as the horse leans on the hand the rider must raise both hands quite sharply upwards to cause the horse to raise its neck and stop leaning (demi-arrêt).

The hands then return to their normal position and keep a light contact with the horse's mouth.
Photos: Laurioux

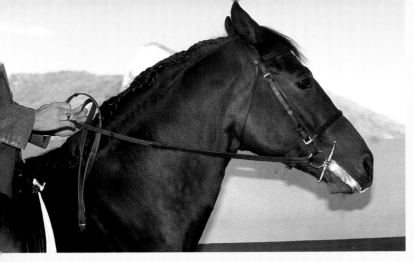

Once the balance and contact have been corrected the work will start again using the normal procedure.

- The legs will only be involved if the horse changes pace: slowing down without being asked.
- Once balance and contact have been corrected the work will start again using the normal procedure: lateral flexion without lowering the head, then poll flexion and slight extension of the neck – with half halt and raising at the slightest sign of any leaning.

The rider bends the horse by slightly lifting the inside hand ...

At the slightest sign of the horse leaning again, the rider corrects it by raising its neck with a demi-arrêt ...

... and then lowers the hand. The horse must bend without lowering the head or leaning on the bit.

...to once again start the normal procedure.
Photos: Laurioux

The rider achieves his goal through an educative approach suited to the specific needs of each horse.

"Overbent" horses

As we have already said, this is the accumulation of several problems.

Depending on the horse, either it drops behind the bit by rounding its neck (high, long and flexible neck), or it overbends by leaning on the hand (short and strong neck).

In both cases we have to start by opening the poll angle and lifting the neck with demi-arrêts so as to restore a natural attitude and a normal contact, then ask the jaw to release without any change in position.

Following this we have to:

• Work a horse that drops behind the bit according to the same progression as a horse with a ewe-neck.
• Work a horse that leans on the bit like a horse in the "leaning on the hand" category.

The young horse is relaxed and flexible, it stretches its top line and carries the rider well.

Overview

We will have been successful because the horse has been educated by a hand that has successively:

• relaxed it and caused the jaw to release...
• made the neck as flexible as we want to supple the whole horse...
• stretched the whole top line by controlling poll flexion and extension of the neck...

All of this has been achieved by educating the horse to the hand and using a rational gymnastics approach without harming the tongue and without compromising forwards movement.

We have achieved what we set out to do (see Alternative, p. 45).

With special cases, we re-establish a good contact by reshaping the neck using methods that are suited to each case, but always in compliance with the fundamental principles: no corrective action on the tongue, no back-wards action with the hand, no opposition between the hands and the legs.

Using these processes we manage to quickly correct cases which initially seem lost causes, which have previously resisted all palliative methods.

It stretches into its reins in all three gaits, releases its mouth and rounds its body.
Photos: Laurioux

An intelligent hand is far better than any type of restrictive training aid.

The most common way of holding the curb and snaffle reins.

The snaffle and curb bits have diametrically opposing effects: *the snaffle lifts-extends, the curb flexes-lowers.*

Holding the reins in the "French" way (top) allows clear separation of the effects of both bits. The official way of holding the reins (bottom) with four permanently adjusted reins, with the snaffle reins held lower than the curb reins in the hand, does not allow the rider to differentiate at all between snaffle and curb.

Double Bridle Work

"Before using the double bridle the rider must learn to use his reins with more subtlety. The aids are given in the same way as in a snaffle bridle, but with even more elasticity in the hands because the leverage on the bit increases the intensity of the action on the mouth." (B1, page 68)

The manual limits itself to these rather vague statements and focuses most of its ideas on describing the different way to hold the reins – without any further explanation.

This is a little meagre.

Do we really use the hands the same way in a double bridle as in a snaffle bridle?

This means that the detrimental effects that have previously been studied will only be amplified – tension, overbending, grinding teeth. Indeed, in spite of the encouragement for more "subtlety" and more "elasticity", we cannot help but notice that crank nosebands are still a major feature.

"More subtlety" is certainly a goal, but firstly in terms of the training philosophy and the concept of the mise en main.

So, we can take a look at the issues involved.

Effects of the double bridle

The full double bridle comprises:

• A snaffle (bridoon) bit: the only bit that can act on the tongue or on the corners of the mouth according to the position of the hand

The bridoon, like a simple snaffle, by acting upwards allows the rider to relax the horse by asking for it to release its jaw and bend, allowing the rider to resist without overbending and lift the neck in a horse that leans or that overbends using demi-arrêts... without the hand moving backwards.

In all these situations the curb bit must not act.

• A curb bit: a bit designed with a leverage effect and a powerful action on the bars, but above all on the tongue... from front to back, whatever position the hand is in.

This is naturally a retroactive bit that is harsh and causes tension. Naturally this means that we must be able to stop it acting at any point in time and take over with the snaffle bit to relax, etc. Once we accept and understand this, the curb bit will only validly contribute to flexing the poll and fixing the head if the horse is constantly and calmly released in its mouth.

When correctly understood, the snaffle and curb bits therefore have diametrically opposing and complementary effects: one is lifting-extending by nature, the other is flexing-lowering by nature, as long as the horse accepts and understands them.

Knowing this, working with four tight reins, and those of the snaffle held lower in the hand than those of the curb, is a rather basic nonsense.

This official way of holding the reins does not allow the rider to differentiate between the snaffle and the curb, nor does it allow him to act separately on either of the bits as required.

In these conditions the rider does not educate the horse to the double bridle, he uses it – and frequently – to have power that he is lacking in a snaffle. Basically we could say that the curb bit in the double bridle is like side reins or draw reins in low hands on a snaffle.

The only difference is that the rider holds the head with four reins instead of two.

Working in a double bridle is only meaningful if it generates even more relaxation, balance and therefore lightness.

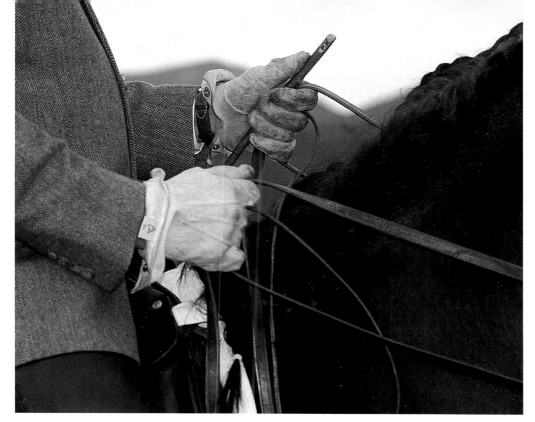

Holding the reins in the French way: the snaffle rein passes over the index finger and the curb rein under the little finger. In order to better distinguish between the two reins the curb rein leaves the hand between the index and middle finger. Photo: Laurioux

Holding the reins

From our previous observations it logically follows that the most effective way to hold the reins, because it is gentle and natural, is using the so-called "French" way. The snaffle rein passes over the index finger and the curb rein under the little finger.

Curiously, the manuals insist on calling this holding the reins in the "Fillis" way. We can wonder why. Certainly, Fillis contributed to the renown of this way of holding them... but on one hand he is not the inventor, and on the other he himself called it the "French" way in his works! (I make this point simply for historical accuracy and not to express any sort of chauvinism.)

It most probably originates in the work of past masters who, to counter the excessive effects of bits with long branches, held the cavesson reins in one hand above the curb hand. What wonderful common sense they had!

The French way of holding the reins probably originates from the work of past masters who took the cavesson reins in one hand held above the curb hand.

In any case it is the only way of holding the reins that allows the rider to separate and combine the effects of the bits both as he desires and instantly.

The infinite number of combinations this offers by playing with your fingers and wrists in a vertical plane remains without any equivalent.

Famous riders of different nationalities have used the French way of holding the reins, here for example Serguei Filatov, James Fillis, Nuno Oliveira and Colonel de Langle de Carry (top to bottom).

Phase 1: To introduce the horse to the double bridle, the rider firstly repeats the flexions already studied in the snaffle bridle, only acting on the snaffle bit with the curb reins hanging loose. Cession de machoire with a high head carriage, etc...

... lateral flexion of the neck, rider placed to the outside...

... then to the inside.
Photos: Laurioux

Introduction to the double bridle

Like the snaffle bridle, the double bridle must not be imposed on the horse, but taught initially in-hand and then under saddle.

Flexions in-hand

• Phase 1: Repeating the flexions already studied in the snaffle bridle whilst only acting on the snaffle bit – curb reins loose.
Whenever the horse releases its jaw it will therefore play with the curb bit and not worry about it.
• Phase 2: Asking for the cession de mâchoire (see glossary) with only the curb bit. With the horse placed straight, its head high and the poll open. The rider stands near the head. Simultaneously and gradually take a contact on both curb reins on a perpendicular line to the head... one forward, the other backward. Without acting on the curb chain, the bit acts on the lower jaw on one side and the upper jaw on the other. Result: the horse cannot avoid opening its mouth. Keep a light contact as long as the horse "tastes the bit".

In the second phase, the rider asks for the cession de mâchoire only using the curb bit and simultaneously and gradually taking a contact on both curb reins on a perpendicular line to the head, one forwards, the other backwards until the horse opens its mouth.

• Phase 3: lateral flexion of the neck. Only on the curb bit (rider placed to the outside).

Repeat the previous cession de mâchoire and push the horse's head into the bend by acting on the outside curb rein, pulled forwards. We can therefore stop any unwanted flexing of the poll.

By combining the snaffle and curb bits: (initially from the outside, this flexion will be repeated with the rider on the inside). Proceed in the same way as with the snaffle bridle, but adding a slight contact on the outside curb rein.

By bending in this way, the horse learns to take a contact in the outside curb rein and release its jaw using a combination of the inside snaffle and the outside curb.

Demi-arrêts (see glossary) on the snaffle reins if the horse tries to flex its poll... otherwise this could lead to overbending.

• Phase 4: poll flexion and extension of the neck.

Phase 3: Lateral flexion of the neck only on the curb. The rider repeats the previous cession de mâchoire and pushes the horse's head into the bend by acting on the outside curb rein, pulled forwards.

Phase 4: For lateral flexions on the snaffle and the curb the rider starts by adding a slight contact on the outside curb rein – initially standing to the outside of the horse...

... then to the inside. Photos: Laurioux

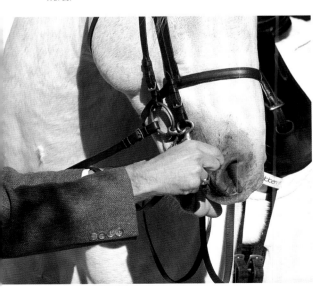

59

Summary of flexions used to introduce the horse to the double bridle: the rider firstly asks for the jaw to release only using the curb bit by taking a contact in both curb reins perpendicularly to the head, one forwards the other backwards.

Then he bends the neck using the same rein action.

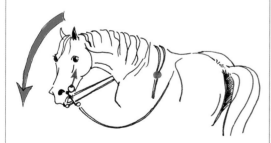

Finally he asks for the flexion by acting upwards on the ring of the inside snaffle whilst the other hand slightly resists on the outside reins to ask the horse to flex its poll. Then he releases and lets the neck lengthen. The horse learns to round and stretch into the outside curb rein.

Increase the bend in the neck using the snaffle whilst slightly resisting on the outside curb rein – the horse flexes its poll. Release and let the neck lengthen whilst staying in the bend and keeping the contact. The horse learns to round himself and stretch himself through the contact with the outside curb rein.

• Phase 5: extension of the neck only on the curb rein.

With the horse placed straight, pass the outside rein over the middle of the neck. Gently take a contact on both reins by bringing together your two hands. Prolong the contact in the reins beyond the cession de mâchoire. When the horse starts to flex the poll, slowly release. Accompany the head downwards and out whilst maintaining a light contact.

This test-flexion is the antidote to overbending.

Phase 5: *The rider teaches the horse to stretch its neck only through the action of the curb.*

As soon as the horse starts to flex the poll, the rider releases...

He passes the outside rein over the middle of the neck and gently takes a contact in both reins by bringing together his two hands.

... and accompanies the head downwards and forwards with both hands whilst maintaining a light contact. Photos: Laurioux

Phase 6: The horse is now ready to work in hand.

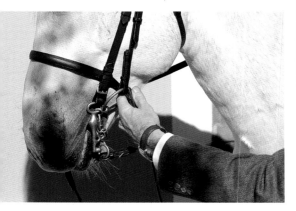

The rider takes the inside reins as close as possible to the bits and held in the "French way".

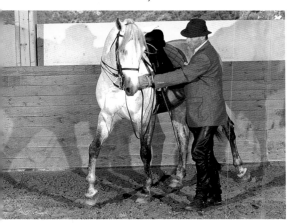

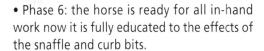

Both outside reins pass over the front of the withers. The rider holds them separated by the index finger and positioned in the middle of the shoulder.

• Phase 6: the horse is ready for all in-hand work now it is fully educated to the effects of the snaffle and curb bits.

The rider will hold the outside reins passing over the front of the withers, separated by the index finger and with the hand positioned in the middle of the shoulder.

In the end, a horse that is perfectly educated to the hand in this way will be able to be controlled by taking both curb reins crossed in one hand just under its chin.

Having reached this stage of training, *the horse will be able to work mainly on the curb reins.*
Photos: Laurioux

The inside reins will be taken as close as possible to the bits and held in the "French" way.

In the end, a horse that is perfectly educated to the bit will be able to be controlled with both curb reins crossed in one hand, held under its chin.

Holding the reins in the French way allows the rider to clearly separate the effects of the curb and the snaffle. In this way he can ask for the cession de mâchoire or use a demi-arrêt to lift the neck and only act on the snaffle.

By slightly lifting the inside hand, he can bend the neck only using the snaffle and adjust the degree of poll flexion via the control obtained through the outside reins.

Asking only with the curb rein, he can stretch the horse's neck down and out.

Flexions under saddle

Repeat the sequence already studied in-hand. Starting with an equal contact in all four reins, the hands on a line between the elbow and the mouth, the rider will be able to:

• Work only on the snaffle, by completely opening the lower fingers on his hand...
• Ask for the cession de mâchoire or use a demi-arrêt that only acts on the snaffle by bending his elbows and lifting the hands...
• Bend the neck using only the snaffle by slightly raising the inside hand and adjust the degree of poll flexion by the control he has through the outside reins: closing the fingers on the curb rein for more flexion, demi-arrêt on the snaffle rein to limit it...
• Stretch the neck by asking only on the curb rein, by rotating and lifting the wrists, and by releasing as the horse takes the reins.

Initially the rider will mostly use the snaffle and will frequently provide support with his hand.

Then as the horse accepts and understands the curb, his actions will increasingly become more discreet.

With the horse remaining relaxed and flexible, the rider will be able to work on shorter reins in more collected attitudes, with the head being increasingly stable.

In the end, the full mise en main (self carriage of the neck, cession de mâchoire and flexing of the poll whilst it remains the highest point) will let the rider work mainly on the curb reins and only use the snaffle for corrective actions.

Lastly, he will be able to present his horse in lightness and only on the curb reins if he feels like it.

Conclusion

Once again, conventional riding tends to focus on a basic approach to usage, rather than on training.

By playing in this way with his fingers and wrists, the rider can act as he needs on the curb or the snaffle. He can ask for lengthening of the neck or a poll flexion using the curb bit...

... or lift the neck using the snaffle.

A full mise en main allows the rider to present his horse only on the curb reins. Photos: Laurioux

If the official dressage manuals only propose an empirical approach to the double bridle and don't explain how to teach it – who will?

Whether educating the horse or training the rider, it is advisable to follow the same progression – moving from known to unknown, and from simple to more complex.

A "low handed" approach to history

In current dressage, the rider who works with low hands will be forgiven everything (including the worst) and be blessed by the system. Conversely, anyone who raises his hands intentionally will be subject to excommunication – all in the name of La Guérinière.

"La Guérinière's teachings still serve as a guideline for today's dressage."
(FN Guidlines for Riding and Driving, German Equestrian Federation vol. 2, p. 15.)
"The German system is mainly based on La Guérinière's teachings." (B2, page 22)
"He liked to use the cavesson with draw reins and used the circle to supple the horse." (B2, page 15)
"Under no circumstances should the rider raise the horse's head by raising his hands."
(FN Guidlines for Riding and Driving, German Equestrian Federation vol. 1, p. 143.)

Let us now examine this "classically orthodox approach" and how loyal it is to La Guérinière:

• **Training aids?**
Whilst draw reins were first used by William Cavendish, *the First Duke of Newcastle*, who used them on the cavesson, whilst they are seen everywhere on Riedinger's engravings and whilst they were introduced to Vienna by Max von Weyrother. La Guérinière mentions neither any training aids nor any authoritarian nosebands, and condemns any solution based on equipment:

Draw reins were first used by the First Duke of Newcastle. *But, although only using them on the cavesson and only to give the bend, they already had some detrimental consequences. La Guérinière condemned all solutions using artificial aids.*

"I deny the utility of bits, spurs and STRAPS, there is nothing outside the rider's resources."

As for suppling on the circle, he above all recommended the use of the "square" and the "volte": at the time a square was traced with two tracks and the shoulder-in was on the straight line!

• **Never lift the front end using the hand?**
La Guérinière writes:

"The height of the hand normally adjusts that of the horse's head; this is why we have to hold it higher than normal for horses that carry their head low in order to LIFT THE NECK…"

• **And low fixed hands?**
La Guérinière wrote:

"The first action, which is to yield and move the hand forwards is a movement that involves LOWERING the hand at the same time as turning the nails a little downwards; the second action is to RAISE the hand, and is done by approaching the hand to the stomach and LIFTING the nails so that they face a little upwards. This last action is used to STOP a horse, to do a DEMI-ARRÊT or even to REIN-BACK."

"… it is easy to notice that a horse that is obedient to the hand is one that follows it in all of its movements."

This portrait of La Guérinière shows the start of a descente de main *through which, following a demi-arrêt, the rider gives the horse "conditional freedom" by lowering the hand. (Showing a portrait by Parrocel taken from "François Robichon de La Guérinière Ecuyer du roi et d'aujourd'hui" Symposium directed by P. Franchet de Esperey, Editions Belin) Draft: Mähler*

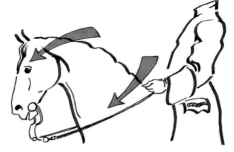

Releasing
→ *forwards*

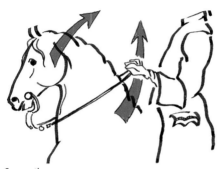

Supporting
→ *Demi-arrêt*
→ *halt*
→ *rein-back*

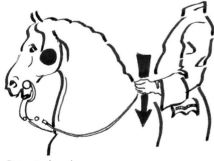

Descente de main
→ *testing balance*

Use of the hand according to La Guérinière:
- *by moving his hand forwards the rider yields and authorises the horse to move forward*
- *by lifting the neck he performs the demi-arrêt, halt or the rein-back.*
- *by the "descente de main" (see glossary), he gives the horse "conditional freedom" and tests its balance.*

• Permanent contact in the reins?
Once again, we can hear what the master has to say on this:

"Take the reins in the right hand, above the left hand and, gradually releasing the reins in the left hand, pass the feeling of the bit into the right hand and lastly, entirely releasing the reins in the left hand, lower the right hand to the horse's neck; the horse now finds itself entirely free, without the curb. This approach to yielding the hand is called the 'DESCENTE DE MAIN' (lowering the hand):
"One of the most subtle and most useful aids in horsemanship."

This is what the master recommends as a test of balance and lightness in the horse: after having done a demi-arrêt (upwards action), leave the horse a little freedom by lowering the hand.

One of his portraits, by Parrocel, is very eloquent in this respect.

The sketches produced by Parrocel show that when training, the riders ask for very pronounced lateral flexions – by raising their hand. (This work is at walk and at a small trot to the left on a volte. Red chalk on cream parchment H0.215; L0.275. Paris, Collection Emile Hermès)

• Bend the horse very little and keep the hand low?

The engravings show a very pronounced bend in the neck.

Indeed the preparatory sketches by PARROCEL show that riders were asking for lateral flexions of almost 90° in their work and by lifting their hand.

Complete disagreement then in every respect.

If modern dressage wanted to go back on everything that La Guérinière stood for, it could not have done any better!

But the good master is not the only one to recommend lifting the neck and raising the hands:

Xenophon (400 BC)

"If we want to have a war horse that attracts people's attention with its magnificent paces, it is important to avoid pulling on its mouth with the brake and using the spur and the whip, by which most people imagine that they can make a horse brilliant... but if we learn to ride our horse with the curb loose, to lift the neck by rounding from the head, we can indeed make it do things happily and proudly."

• Raising of the neck, flexion at the top of the poll and descente de main: everything is there!

Charles Dupaty de Clam (1744-1782), The Science and Art of Equitation, 1776

"Not every horse is gifted with good conformation by nature in order for our Art to quickly give them a beautiful attitude..."

"We can get there in the end after getting the horse to bring up its nose: there is no risk in giving this attitude until the neck strengthens and supports itself since the end of the nose will always fall back sufficiently to the vertical."

• Baucher's "second manner" could not say it better.

Ludwig Hünersdorf (1748-1813), The Most Natural and Easiest Method for Schooling Horses, 1791

"Flexions" "... gradually we will try to lift the head and neck more by gradually lifting the hand. In this way we will gradually arrive at a height that the horse will get used to carrying its head with."

"Of the action of the hands" "When the rider pulls his hands backwards and upwards to lift the forehand he must put them gradually back as soon as the effect is obtained in order to release the primary tension in the reins."

Hünersdorf often refers to La Guérinière, but at least it is obvious that he has read and understood him!

François Faverot de Kerbrech (1837-1905) Methodic Schooling of the Saddle Horse according to the Last Teachings of F. Baucher, collected by one of his students, 1891.

"Jaw Flexions" "... taking one snaffle rein in each hand, the rider starts by lifting the neck and head as far as possible using demi-arrêts if necessary; then he asks for lightness through a slight, equal and continuous contact in the reins upwards and from front to back, so that the bit only acts on the corners of the mouth."

"Of the demi-arrêt" "When a horse has a strong tendency to drop its neck, we must hold our wrists very high above the ears if necessary until the jaw gently releases in this position."

"Of the descente de main" "...with the animal light and with its head placed, open the left hand and lower the right hand holding the end of the reins down to the neck."

• Sometimes La Guérinière and Baucher go "hand in hand"!

To correct a horse that has a dead mouth and that refuses to release, Waldemar Seunig recommends lifting the inside hand to the height of the horse's ears.

*As shown in this famous portrait, **Louis Seeger** was neither a fan of low hands, nor of paroxystic flexion of the poll, nor of authoritarian nosebands.*

Changes of Direction

The official theory

This can be summarised as follows: the horse must only turn by taking an overall bend that is exactly the same as the curve of the circle on which it is on. And all of the sketches show horses perfectly matching the curves from their ears to their tails, like a train on rails.

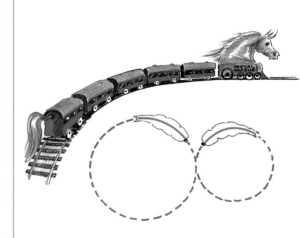

According to official theory, the horse must only turn with an overall bend that exactly matches the curve of the circle it is on.

Waldemar Seunig (1887–1976)

In his work entitled *Am Pulsschlag der Reitkunst (The Pulse of Horsemanship)* this author recommends raising the inside hand to the height of the horse's ears to correct a subject with a dead mouth that refuses to release. Unfortunately, he does not try to explain the phenomenon and therefore it remains a "trick". This is a shame, because he may have been tempted to look at the principles and generalise the process... that is typical of Baucher's "Second Manner".

Louis Seeger (1799–1860)

It is difficult to say that his famous equestrian portrait can be used to recommend low hands, authoritarian nosebands and paroxystic flexion of the poll!

Whatever the official theory says, La Guérinière had much more in common with F. Baucher's *Second Manner* than with today's dressage.

The horse's neck cannot be thought of as a bicycle's handlebars, but should instead be seen as a balancing pole that the rider can use to change the balance.

In these conditions, the rider uses the neck like a cyclist uses the handlebars.

So, why not look at the horse without any prejudice in terms of doctrine: it will certainly give us the best solution!

• Clue n°1:

Left to themselves, horses virtually always turn by putting their head to the outside.
It would therefore seem that a counter-bend is the most favourable posture for changing direction.

• Clue n°2:

On the lunge or ridden, a young horse naturally bent to the right, spontaneously goes on a bigger circle to the right than to the left. This confirms the previous observation.

• Clue n°3:

On a straight line a horse, naturally bent to the right, does not stay on one track… it moves towards the left shoulder and consequently its haunches escape to the right.

Conclusion

For a given bend, a horse always more easily weights its outside shoulder.

Resistance in the left rein has two inseparable causes: contraction of the muscles on the right hand side of the neck and weighting of the left shoulder. Consequently the ideal corrective exercise would involve combining a lateral flexion to the left and moving the shoulders to the right – in other words: turning in a counter-bend.

The neck cannot be thought of as a bicycle's handlebars, but more as a balancing pole, and turning it should not be considered a mechanical problem but more like a change in balance.

Fundamentally, the horse turns by moving its shoulders to the right or to the left of the line of the haunches, and not by bending (we will come back to this).

All of this means that, to change direction, the most natural aid involves pushing the neck towards the inside shoulder whilst bending it to the outside. This is by definition what we call a neck-rein.

Indeed, what could be more logical than modifying the weight distribution between the two shoulders by a sideways movement of the hand?

In this case, there is no opposition to the forwards movement and there is no need to compensate with your legs – saving effort because when you do the right thing, you can do less.

All working equitation methods use the neck-rein. Western riding is a good example of this.

The opening rein: after giving the bend, the rider turns his wrist, nails upwards, and opens the hand away from the neck to encourage the horse to move to the side.

Official equitation once again confuses the end and the means. Whilst bending the neck exactly in the axis of movement is a valid presentation objective, it naturally should not be the only way of using the neck throughout the horse's schooling.

The neck-rein: to turn to the right whilst keeping the left bend, the rider presses the left rein against the neck.

If necessary he can help the horse to understand by opening the right rein. Photos: Laurioux

Schooling the horse to the neck-rein

A horse that is naturally bent to the right will react spontaneously to the right neck-rein because it confirms its natural tendency, but it must be educated to respond to the left neck-rein.

Phase 1

• On the right rein on the track, give a bend to the left and maintain this through the corners by turning your nails upwards and pressing the left rein against the neck. Weight the right side and if necessary help the horse to understand by opening the right rein.

• As soon as the horse goes well into the corner in this way, carry on for a few strides coming off the track, then for a whole volte.

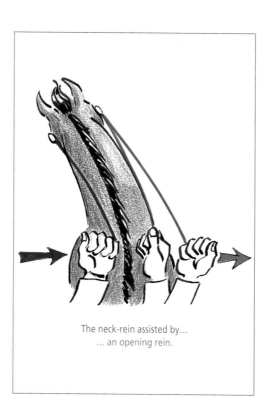

The neck-rein assisted by…
… an opening rein.

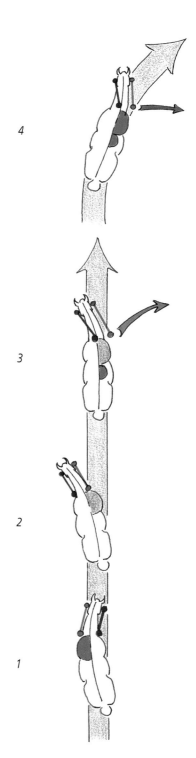

A horse that is hollow to the right weights his left shoulder and leans on the left rein (1). Bending to the left shifts part of the weight to the right shoulder but the horse's haunches continue to escape (2). By pressing the left rein against the neck and weighting the right seat, the rider brings the shoulders back in front of the haunches (3) and turns in a counter-bend (4). The weight is then distinctly shifted back to the right shoulder. If necessary, the rider assists the left neck-rein by opening the right rein.

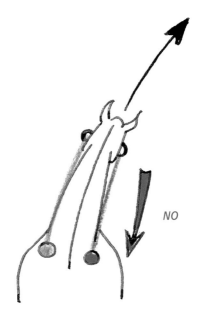

The inside "hand-brake" rein.

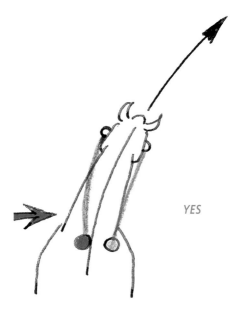

The outside "balancing pole" rein.

The correct use of the reins in changing direction. *The rider must not use the inside rein as a "hand-brake" but instead act by pressing the outside rein to move the shoulders in the direction of the turn.*

• Very quickly the horse will be able to trace figures of eight and serpentines without changing bend.

Phase 2

• Once it knows the neck-rein effect, the horse will then be able to respond to this independently of the bend.
• The rider will be able to turn to the right with a bend to the right using a left neck-rein. This is the correct use of the outside rein... instead of holding on the left whilst pulling on the right, like we see too often.
• He could also move out on the circle simply using an inside neck-rein, or move in on the circle with an outside neck-rein.

Phase 3

By shifting the shoulders to the right, lightening the left shoulder and weighting the right shoulder in a left bend, the neck-rein is the most effective, simple and natural way of straightening a horse that is bent to the right with haunches escaping to the right – at all paces, and particularly at canter.

A little more history, concerning turning

Modern dressage only looks at turning in terms of the "bending of the whole backbone".

It focuses on the priority role of the legs to bend the dorsal segment (a question that will be dealt with further on) and does not recommend any particular rein action. We can see what our spiritual guide, La Guérinière, has to say about this:

"The hand must always start the first action, and the legs must accompany this movement because it is a general principle that in all gaits, both natural and artificial, the horse's head and shoulders must be in front of the haunches."

So, we again have the supremacy of the hand.

"The third action of the hand is to turn right, by moving the hand to this side with the nails turned a little upwards in order for the outside rein, which is the left rein, the one which must carry out the action, to act more promptly."
"The fourth action is to turn left. Moving the hand that way, turning the nails down a little, in order to act on the outside rein, which is the right rein on this occasion."
"We can also note that when we use the outside rein by moving the hand towards the inside, this action causes the outside shoulder to move inwards and makes the outside leg move over the inside one: and when we use the inside rein, moving the hand towards the outside, this movement widens the inside shoulder, in other words it makes the inside leg move over the outside one. We can see, that through these different inside and outside rein actions, that it is what we do with our hands that controls the horse's forehand..."

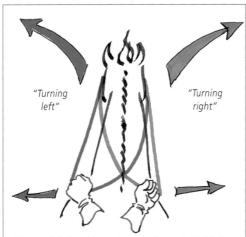

The use of the hand in turning according to La Guérinière: *To turn left the rider moves his hand to the left with his nails downwards: to turn right he moves his hand to the right with his nails upwards. The outside neck-rein causes the horse to change direction.*

In other words, the neck-rein.

All in all, this is an outright rejection: no reference to overall bend, no particular role for the legs... priority to the hand and the use of lateral actions: the "neck-rein".

And our good master then provides *the coup de grace*:

"... any rider who does not know the use of the curb reins works without rule or principle."

> In terms of changing direction, Western riding is much closer than official dressage to La Guérinière's teachings.

Lastly, the writings of Faverot de Kerbrecht allow us to again look at the last teachings of Baucher, the black sheep of well-to-do dressage.

"Turning on small circles using the outside neck-rein."
"If with this action, and the jaw remaining soft, the end of the horse's nose turns slightly to the outside of the circle, the weight of the neck is shifted to the inside."
"A way of straightening a horse."
"It is the shifting of the weight from one shoulder to the other, by using the neck-rein, that consequently bends the horse in the opposite direction to its initial direction... but these directions must be obtained only by the hand."

Overview

Official dressage positions itself as the guardian of the temple of classical equitation, sacrificing itself to the cult of La Guérinière and burning Baucher, the impostor.

However, from beginning to end the fundamental question of the use of the hand shows that La Guérinière's precepts obviously match the last teachings of Baucher and that they totally disagree with the dressage manuals. The accumulation of so many falsehoods is nothing short of fraudulent.

To redress the balance, and not without a little irony, we could paraphrase Seeger's "Serious warnings to dressage riders". By claiming its heritage from La Guérinière, this discipline is awarding itself a diploma in classicism and assuming the most flattering of historical legacies. However, these titles are not well deserved since it is the exact opposite both in principle and in practice.

The great master from the Tuileries Riding School could have concluded: "You are never betrayed as well as by your own".

Conclusion

Modern dressage fails to talk about the hand, as if it is hiding an ugly illness, and boils everything down in this respect to rather cloudy considerations on the predominance of the seat, back and legs. The instructor therefore treats the hand as an accessory, something to be despised, whereas his attitude only has one true cause: he has no idea what to say about it!

There is no doubt that a beautiful position and a good seat are essential, but they do not suffice - far from it. Even Steinbrecht, whose teachings on the hand tend more to be an invitation to authority than to subtlety, warns us in this respect:

"A rider who has a truly good hand is a master of equitation, even when his position and the way he behaves on horseback may make him appear an unskilled rider to the layman. Conversely, a rider with a really bad hand will never be a rider in the true sense of the word, however appealing he is through the strength of his seat, his reputation and his elegance, since his failing can only come from a lack of sense and understanding of the horse. "

Nobody has ever denied the virtue of a "good hand". It is defined: "supple, firm, elastic, sensitive, etc.". But these are truisms which provide little information, like saying "It's better to be rich and healthy than poor and ill".

As to "How?", it can be resumed in the leitmotif: "fixed and low hands"... and we know the extremes that this leads to more often than not: using force, authoritarian nosebands, training aids, overbending, etc.

When it is well understood, dressage boils down to the rider's natural talent and the horse's aptitudes. It must state what makes a good hand, without being esoteric, and explain:

- how we educate the horse to it...
- how we teach it to the rider...
- how we judge it in competitions.

From the above study, we can produce intelligible definitions, clear principles and reliable methods, both for schooling horses and for training riders.

The horse "en main"

The definition owes as much to La Guérinière as to Baucher: this is a horse that releases its mouth softly and loyally accompanies the hand wherever it moves.

> The horse "en main" has a mouth that releases the bit, attached to a neck that is always ready to bend, stretch or grow without resistance.

The "mise en main" cannot be limited to a position, even if it is correct... its definition is of variable geometry.

The mise en main

The horse needs a gradual education to the hand and its effects, like a student needs to learn to use his hands intelligently.

The rider balances and works his horse gymnastically by using its neck instead of using palliative methods to stop it using it against the rider.

> The mise en main is something that focuses on the hand... and only the hand. The use of force or coercive instruments is excluded by definition. Tight nosebands and training aids are prohibited.

Stability

Submission to the reins must not result from a fight between the horse's neck and the rider's arms, but from a dialogue between firstly the mouth and secondly the hand.

The first duty of the hand is to accompany the mouth in all of its movements so that it does not force any attitude.

Consequently, the famous fixed hand must above all be fixed relative to the mouth rather than the back. It only becomes fixed relative to the back when, with progress, the mise en main stabilises the head.

> It is not the hand that seeks to impose stability of the head, but the head that authorises the rider to gradually fix the hand.
> Riding your horse with a fixed hand is therefore an objective, but it must under no circumstances be used as a means of training.

Chronological sequence for the mise en main

Relaxation being a preliminary to any valid work, the hand must do the following, in order of priority:

- relax by causing a cession de mâchoire
- make the horse flexible by bending its neck as required
- encourage poll flexion and neck extension

Once this initial stage in the mise en main is confirmed, the gradual raising of the neck and increased poll flexion will accompany the overall gymnastic progress.

> In order, the rider takes possession firstly of the mouth, then the neck and lastly the poll.
> We cannot change the sequence of this progression without causing damage – as is eloquently shown by the overbent horse.

Use of the hand

The hand must do what we expect of it efficiently and whilst respecting the mouth. As a consequence:

- Holding the reins: the hand adjusts the reins by positioning itself on the line between the rider's elbow and horse's mouth (natural attitude). Apart from the thumb and the index finger, that set the length of rein, the fingers remain half open on the reins.
- Corrective actions, that will be needed during any learning process, must be applied to the corners of the mouth and under no circumstances to the tongue. They must therefore be via an upwards action on the snaffle or the bridoon.

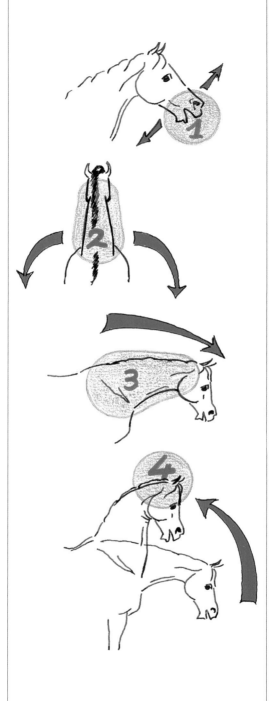

Chronological sequence of the mise en main: the rider must firstly relax the horse by causing the jaw to release; then make it flexible by bending its neck as required; this will encourage the extension of the neck. Flexing the poll will only be approached at the same time as lifting the neck.

• Acting on the tongue, with the snaffle or the curb is only conceivable if the horse is relaxed, or if the horse continues to be released in its mouth. The rule must simply be contact rather than leaning.

• The rider's ongoing objective is to gradually reduce the actions of the hands to simply playing with his fingers and wrists.

The hand can act:

• By closing the fingers and slowly raising both hands to get the jaw to release…

• By slowly raising one single hand for lateral flexion of the neck.

• By brief and repeated raising of the hand to transfer weight to the rear: demi-arrêt, halts, rein-back…

• By lateral actions: moving against the neck (neck-rein) or opening (opening rein), to transfer weight from one shoulder to another.

The hand releases by opening the fingers and coming back to its initial position (descente de main). It yields by moving forward towards the mouth or by letting the reins become longer.

> The hand plays its role every time it allows the horse to work with a released mouth and a stable head in a *descente de main.*

Dressage rules

• Double or reinforced nosebands should be prohibited. Riding without a noseband should be allowed and even encouraged.

• Mobility of the jaw must be integrated in the scores for each figure. A correct front end must be more important than precision: a volte that is a little too big or small, but with a released mouth should be given a better score than an accurate volte ridden with a horse that is leaning on the hand.

• Any protests about the hand: the tongue pulled back, to the side, over the bit, and grinding of teeth must be penalised for each figure.

• Tests should include a large diversity of figures combined with many variations of attitudes (bend, counter-bend, extension and raising of the neck), that are carefully sequenced. This would then get rid of horses that are just drilled and riders who practise like mad at the last minute and would reward flexible horses and sensitive riders.

Anthropologists accept that during his evolution, man has developed his brain in synergy with the morphological evolution of his hand (all of this related to standing upright). Without this intelligent hand he could not have invented, written, drawn, painted, sculpted, produced music… or developed equestrian art.

> Any training approach that only gives the hand a subordinate role will be forced to use coercive and vulgar solutions. It becomes sidetracked and leads to cultural regression.

Without a doubt "the limits of lightness lie in the rider's talent" (de Salins) and not everyone has the same natural gifts – nonetheless, anybody, even those of modest talent, who have understood a rational use of the hand, will easily improve horses that have failed with professionals.

> "A hard bit has the effect of constraining a horse whereas we have to stop it from hurting him. We can only succeed with a gentle bit and above all an intelligent hand: since the bit is the hand and a nice hand is the whole rider." (Baucher)

An intelligent hand can make a prodigy

> "Art is beautiful when the head, the heart and the hand work together"
> (J. Ruskin)

THE LEGS

Official drawing
Compliments of the author

This drawing from the dressage manual shows a horse which, in collected trot, flexes its haunches and shortens its frame whilst propelling itself energetically in trot towards the rider's hand: "In collection, there is increased flexion of the haunches. The hind legs move further under the body (in the direction of the centre of gravity)". (B1, page 149)
The green silhouette, added by the author, shows the natural weight-bearing base.

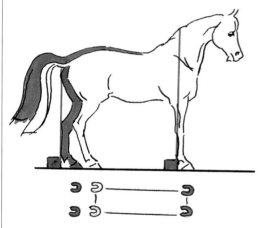

The horse shortens its frame by a durable flexion of the lumbar back, which holds the hind legs under the body. This shortens the weight-bearing base from the rear.

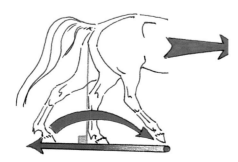

The horse develops its propulsive force by moving forward. However, it is the extension of the weight-bearing hind leg, which propels the mass or in other words its disengagement.

As outstanding propulsive aids, the legs are the driving force of a healthy approach to riding.
They have the following functions:

• developing the "propulsive power" of the hind legs by working in forwards movement
• maintaining "costal flexion" in all work executed on curves or in all lateral work
• "engaging the hind legs in the direction of the centre of gravity" in all transitions... and in the end for collection.

Controlling the horse's activity, flexibility and balance – the legs are very important aids. We can look a little closer at their nobility!

Forwards movement

Propulsive force

"Developing the propulsive force"
"Developing the propulsive power means both stimulating the hind legs, making them work more actively and strengthening their engagement under the body in the direction of the centre of gravity."
"The frame of the horse shortens with the development of the propulsive force and engagement of the hind legs under the body." (FN Guidelines for Riding and Driving German Equestrian Federation, vol. 1, page 142.)

This theory of the shortening of the horse's frame by jointly developing the "propulsive force of the hindquarters" and their "engagement under the horse's body" is very appealing to the mind, but it does not withstand analysis.

We can review the situation: a horse shortens its frame through durable flexion of the lumbar back which holds the hind legs under the body, which shortens its weight-bearing base from the rear.

It is naturally through forwards movement that the rider develops the "propulsive force" of his horse.

However, it is the extension of the weight-bearing hind leg which propels the mass, or in other words its disengagement.

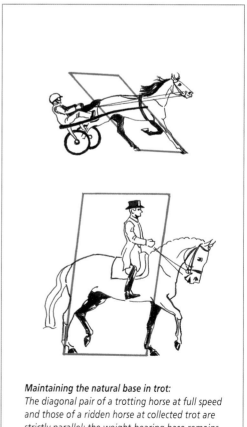

Maintaining the natural base in trot:
The diagonal pair of a trotting horse at full speed and those of a ridden horse at collected trot are strictly parallel: the weight-bearing base remains unchanged. The dressage horse has therefore shortened its stride, but not its frame.

Propulsive forces do lower the haunches, but this is by extending the lumbar back and pulling the hind legs out beyond their natural plumb line (frame which lengthens), the opposite of the official theory.

If we compare the diagonal pairs of a trotting horse at full speed and those of a saddle horse at collected trot, the limbs remain strictly parallel in both cases. The dressage horse has therefore shortened its stride but not its frame.

In summary:

• The more a horse lengthens its stride the more it develops its "propulsive force" and the less it can shorten its frame.
• However energetic they are, strides which shorten do not give any gain in terms of "engagement of the hind legs under the mass".
• In terms of locomotion, "development of the propulsive force" and "engagement of the hind legs under the body" are absolutely incompatible. Whatever the rider does, as long as the horse is moving frankly forwards it cannot "shorten its frame".

This concept of the horse which shortens its base due to the engagement of the hindquarters resulting from the development of their propulsive force is one of the dogmas of modern dressage. The laws of locomotion disprove it categorically.

The official drawing showing a horse which flexes its haunches and shortens its propulsive base energetically in trot towards the rider's hand, illustrates the obsession of a system, but in no way resembles reality.

Natural bases

Study of locomotion clearly shows: "development of the propulsive force" and "shortening of the bases" are absolutely incompatible. In a dressage horse at extended trot the natural weight-bearing base is maintained: the horse's frame is not shortened.

Natural bases

On the contrary, a horse may propel itself by lengthening the lumbar back and moving its hind legs backwards beyond their natural plumb line: therefore lengthening its frame.

Schwung and impulsion

> "Schwung is of good quality if the hocks are energetically carried forwards and upwards, immediately after the foot has left the ground."
>
> "Schwung is only possible in trot and canter. There can be no schwung in walk, because there is no moment of suspension." (B1, page 139)

Equestrian vocabulary varies from one language to another when it comes down to designating the quality of forwards movement.

In German it is 'schwung', in French and English 'impulsion'. These terms are not synonymous. We can try to clarify this.

If we compare two situations:

• Horse No 1: has a spectacular medium trot with energetic strides and a long moment of suspension. This under a rider who has to constantly push with strong legs.
• Horse No 2: moves simply from halt to working trot, but without the slightest hesitation, and under a rider whose legs act imperceptibly.

Question: which of these two horses is better schooled?

Nobody would ever hesitate to answer: No 2.

But No 1 showed schwung and No 2 showed impulsion. So we can say...

• Horse No 1 has a naturally high quality trot, which indeed it expresses just as well or even better at liberty. But its future schooling is limited because true collection will remain inaccessible unless it is seriously educated to the legs.
• Horse No 2 has excellent schooling, showing great lightness to the legs. Although nature has not given it a very expressive trot, with

this amount of impulsion and through collection, the rider will be able to stylise the paces and produce schwung in the end.

In the end, schwung above all shows a natural aptitude, an aspect of horse breeding which can therefore be bought "off-the-shelf". Conversely, impulsion corresponds to a degree of responsiveness, which results from education.

Since we are talking about schooling here, we should therefore focus on impulsion.

Definition of impulsion

The activity, or even the expression of the gaits, is not sufficient to define impulsion. It depends on the degree of obedience to the legs and is therefore dependent on the horse's responsiveness.

We can express this as follows:

$$\text{Impulsion} = \frac{\text{horse's response}}{\text{rider's request}}$$

This equation helps us see that impulsion can be increased in two ways:

• by increasing the horse's activity, with a constant level of request from the rider's legs.

$$\text{Impulsion} \uparrow = \frac{\text{activity} \uparrow}{\text{legs} \rightarrow}$$

• by lowering the intensity of the action of the legs, with a constant level of response from the horse.

$$\text{Impulsion} \uparrow = \frac{\text{activity} \rightarrow}{\text{legs} \downarrow}$$

However we know that: $\frac{1}{0} = \text{infinity}$

So we can see that it is vain to believe that we can improve impulsion, and therefore the horse's schooling, by constantly maintaining the movement, or even by asking for more activity using stronger legs.

And yet this is the advice from the dressage manual:

> "For horses that do not answer brief aids, the rider must make the horse more reactive, initially by using stronger aids." (B1, page 63)

Whilst the hand acts directly on the mouth through the reins, there is no physical link between the rider's legs and the horse's hind legs. Horses are not born with small sensor-accelerators usefully built into their sides just behind the girth.

Simply ride a young horse in its early training to measure this; not only do the legs have no natural vocation for putting the horse forward, but they even have an increasingly inhibitive effect according to the intensity with which they are used. It is in the horse's deepest nature that when gripped by someone with a leg on each side of its back, it will react as if being attacked by a predator: the horse tenses or tries to get rid of the intruder and does not go into a wonderful canter! In this case a horse will consider spurs to be like a predator's claws... they will increase the impression of being attacked.

By using the leg and spur like mad without any result, a rider easily concludes that his horse is lazy or insensitive, even though his mount's skin will react perfectly well if a fly lands on it!

"We must not take all of a horse's faults to be vices; since most of the time they come from ignorance, and often weakness."
(La Guérinière)

A rider using "more" legs when a horse does not react is like a teacher who shouts a word because the student does not understand it - simply adding the grotesque to the inefficient!

> **Impulsion can only result from careful education to the language of the legs.**

The lesson of the leg

Fearful by nature, the horse has a strong flight instinct. The rider must use it. Any element of surprise, especially when it comes from outside of its visual field, causes immediate flight in the horse. For this reason we must use the whip and not spurs.

"...we should notice that the purpose of hitting a horse with a whip, when well applied and at the right time, is to make a lot more of an impression on a naughty horse and to chase it forward, compared with those riders who use their spurs or who punish it."
(La Guérinière)

Having said that, a whip should be considered an aid. The rider must make sure that his horse respects it and to achieve this the horse needs to understand it rather than fear it. Before using the whip at all, the rider must be able to touch the horse over its whole body whilst it remains calm and motionless.

Pavlov gave the definitive demonstration of creating a conditioned reflex. By applying these methods with intelligence and rigour we obtain quick and surprising results.

In principle this involves:

• adding a natural stimulus (causing the result we want) to an artificial stimulus (to be taught)

• repeating this often, enhancing each positive response with a reward

• particularly rewarding the tendency to anticipate (no longer needing the natural stimulus)

• when the stimuli substitution is complete, periodically strengthening this by returning to the natural stimulus every time the reflex loses its sharpness.

Method applied to the lesson of the leg.
1. Very light pressure of the lower leg (at most, enough to squash a fly) must lead to a frank and immediate acceleration.
2. If this is not the case, the pressure of the legs is prolonged and within a second, the whip is used decisively (tapping with increasing frequency and intensity until a lively reaction is obtained).
3. Let the horse express itself, with the rider ceasing any other action: "release the legs". After going at most once around the school, stop the horse and praise. Leave the horse to rest, reins at the buckle.
4. Repeat the process until the horse anticipates the effect of the whip. Do not use the whip, and reward generously.
5. Any unrequested slowing must cause an immediate reminder, not from the leg, but from the whip.

Acting in this way we can get a horse to strike off to canter from halt simply by bringing the legs close to its side, in a few minutes, even if it is reputed to be an impossibly insensitive and lazy horse. But there are also certain precautions to take:

• The horse's understanding and responsiveness to the leg mean that the rider must not oppose its effects with any action of the hand. The development of Baucher's concepts in this respect is exemplary. His "First Manner" was based on the "effet d'ensemble" (see glossary): "continuous and correctly opposed forces between the hands and legs"; with this

Collection according to Baucher's First Manner led to the so-called "goat on a mountain top" position.

effect having "the goal of bringing back all parts of the horse that move out of a position of balance". Whilst this process quickly brought about complete submission from the horse without any violence, it led to artificial collection due to neck carriage that was too low and the converging of the limbs under the horse's body (the so-called "goat on a mountain top" position). All of this was prejudicial to impulsion and many students, when left to themselves or without enough experience, produced horses that almost refused to go forward. General L'Hotte wrote concerning the "First Manner" that the rider "...would have nothing in his hand but would carry his horse with his legs". As part of his on-going research, Baucher arrived at his "Second Manner", which is unfortunately not very well known. It is based, among other innovations, on the principle of *"hand without legs, legs without hand"*.

"By avoiding the simultaneous use of the hand and the legs, the horse will more clearly understand what we want from it and the rider will be obliged to be more careful in the use of his aids because all of the mistakes he makes will be seen fully and straight away."
(François Baucher)

The "effet d'ensemble" is only taught at a later stage and is only used exceptionally to eliminate any disobedience.

• The lesson of the leg can only be given by a rider with a stable leg. Legs that are tight, gripping or constantly moving are unsuitable. They are constantly "talking for no purpose" and form a "background noise" which makes the horse switch off.

• In order to keep its impulsive value, the leg must only be used to produce extra forwards movement. This naturally excludes it from participating in slowing down, stopping or reining back.

• In order to ask for a high level of forwards movement, the leg must not act more, but must limit itself to acting for longer (with over-sensitive horses) or repeating its basic pressure until the required result is obtained (with phlegmatic horses).

• Be very demanding, but very brief, with breaks in between at full rest (reward and time to think). Nothing is more detrimental to developing impulsion than long sequences, endless kilometres and drilling. Once obedience to the legs is well established we have to give the "lesson of the spur", just as we initiated the horse to the whip. Without preliminary education, most horses react to spurs by holding themselves back and even stopping, since the action of the spur can cause contraction of the underbelly muscles (thorax and abdomen). Spurs must never be used to force obedience to incorrectly educated legs.

> **"Nothing disappoints and demeans a horse more than spurs that are used too often and inappropriately."** *(La Guérinière)*

The rider will therefore initially look for a horse that remains calm and motionless on a frank and prolonged contact of the spurs (gentle spurs, especially with very sensitive horses). This is the "mise á l'éperon" (educating to the spur) as recommended by F. Baucher. Once fear and contractions are eliminated, the rider can teach the horse the meaning of the spurs by associating them with the whip.

The true role of spurs is either to take the place of the whip with more variety and precision via "attacks", or to be the most subtle expression of the leg, an extension of it used with delicate touches: the so called "pinches" which "electrify" the horse.

Conclusion

Conventional equestrian teaching tends to be focussed on this all-too-often repeated statement: "Ride on! Stronger! More legs! More legs!"

And everyone admires and gives compliments to a rider who "rides strongly".

This focus on virility hides a major misunderstanding of the horse and produces a muscular and laborious style of riding.

The horse's work

One of the goals of dressage is for the rider to act with fewer and fewer aids.

If its education is carried out properly the horse becomes "light to the legs" and can be ridden as often as possible with the descente de jambes (see glossary - legs that are relaxed and that drape down the horse's side from top to bottom).

A horse with impulsion is mentally in the "starting blocks" - it seems to go forward

The rider's aids have nothing to do with force – the horse is not a bicycle that needs you to pedal harder in order to accelerate.

The horse is light to the leg when it is mentally in the "starting blocks".

before the rider, asks and never lowers its work rate on its own initiative. La Guérinière had a nice way of talking about this: "The will to go!"

A horse that is well schooled is "light to the legs".

Teachers would be better off giving the *"Whys"* and *"Hows"* instead of saying *"Stronger!"* and *"More!"* They should be capable of explaining and showing the *"lesson of the leg"* and then have their students give this lesson. This would avoid the unpleasant sight of dulled horses ridden by sweating riders - and would also avoid them shouting for nothing!

Competition

Riders who turn up with spur marks on their horses, or horses with bare patches where the leg rubs, should be sent away to study more.

When we take part in a dressage test the idea is to arrive with a horse that is already schooled. Obedience to the legs is elementary and fundamental, and therefore the whip should not be authorised, even in the warm up. This would avoid us having to watch unpleasant last minute settling, of scores between the horse and rider.

"Lightness to the leg" should be marked. Raised heels and the permanent use of spurs should be penalised for each figure.

It is not acceptable for two identical transitions from halt to trot to receive the same score when one is achieved by force and spurs and the other with discreet, relaxed legs. By not making these distinctions we promote an empirical use of the horse rather than dressage.

Overall bend

Overall bend, the bending of the whole horse around the rider's inside leg is one of the key points of modern dressage.

"The rider must avoid asking for too much bend of the neck and should focus on the costal flexion around his inside leg." (B1, page 63)

"Overall bend of the horse will increase as the diameter of the circle decreases and collection will consequently increase." (B2, page 31) (B1, page 110)

The focus on "costal flexion" is very much due to G. Steinbrecht and his book, *The Gymnasium of the Horse:*

"Through this a horse can correctly follow curved lines, promptly and easily turn short and tightly and hold itself on two tracks with distinct and flowing paces."
"Flexion of the ribs is therefore the core of all riding and riders should give it the same attention as flexion of the neck, if they do not want to feel something is missing every lesson, or even every stride." (pp. 105 and 106)
"The rider should therefore mainly focus on flexing the ribs and use the latter to accordingly dose that of the forehand in order for the entire spine to be uniformly bent." (p. 150)

We can forget any dogmatic prejudice we may have and try to stick to the facts as taught by the horse, the most impartial of all masters.

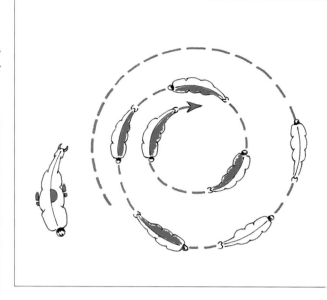

Overall bend, the bending of the whole horse around the rider's inside leg, is one of the key points of modern dressage: the horse is meant to match the overall bend of its whole spine to the curve of the circle it is on.

Anatomy

The degree of freedom of the dorso-lumbar segment of the horse is extremely limited. This is one of the reasons that make it possible to ride. If the horse had a cat's spine, it would be very flexible, it would jump much higher... but it would be impossible to ride. Whatever the rider does, he cannot ask for more than nature can give.

Harry Boldt's book, *The Dressage Horse* shows dozens of photographs taken from above the horse. We can make the following observations:

• On all of the photographs dorsal flexion is virtually non-existent.
• On all of the photographs, the neck is bent distinctly more than the rest of the spine.

Even in the shoulder-in at trot, dorsal flexion is virtually invisible – the horse always bends the neck much more than the dorso-lumbar segment (sketch of a photo taken from The Dressage Horse *by Harry Boldt).*

• Even in the best of exercises for "costal flexion" (shoulder-in at trot) and at the most favourable point in time (extension of the outside diagonal), the dorso-lumbar segment only shows an imperceptible degree of bending.

Both the horse's anatomy and these photographs show that this famous "costal flexion" is virtually non existent, or only very slight at most.

Misleading feelings

If we look at what happens in the closing phase of the right lateral pair and the opening phase of the left lateral pair at walk or trot, we note the following:

• The lumbo-sacral joint has no latero-flexion, but the rotation of the dorsal and lumbar vertebrae combine during the weight-bearing phase of the left hind leg and the engaging of the right hind leg, the hips pivot to the right while at the same time the left haunch rises whilst the right one drops.
• At the moment when the limbs of the right lateral pair converge, the right shoulder and thigh come closer together, compressing the thorax and the abdomen and pushing them to the left. This is especially easy since this is the point in time when the limbs of the left lateral pair are moving apart.
• These pendulum movements of the torso are linked to a slight latero-flexion of one part of the dorso-lumbar segment (from D9 to L4) associated with twisting of the whole area (slight rotation of the vertebrae relative to one another).

It is the addition of this: vertebral twisting + rotation of the hips + reflux of the torso which amplifies the movement of the dorso-lumbar segment and pushes the rider's left leg and attracts the right leg. This gives him the impression of a large amount of latero-flexion. However, in fact it is not only very limited, it is also periodic.

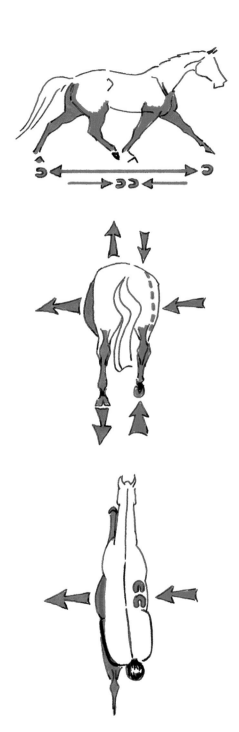

During the closing phase of the right lateral pair, the horse's right haunch drops and the left one rises. The thorax and abdomen move to the left. This gives the rider an illusion of a high degree of latero-flexion to the right.

Locomotion

Although the lateral movement of the dorso-lumbar segment remains limited, it is still real. In all vertebrates the movement of the limbs depends on periodic undulations of the spine since these control the action of the muscles which move the shoulders and the haunches. In canter, the rachis moves mainly in the vertical plane (like a dolphin swimming); at walk and trot in the horizontal plane (like a fish swimming).

Conclusion: under no circumstances can the horse maintain a posture in which the dorso-lumbar segment is bent in movement.

We can also look at what happens on a circle to the right at trot. The stride can be broken down into two phases.

1. Right diagonal pair bearing weight whilst the left one is in flight: the right lateral pair closes whereas the left one opens. This is the ideal phase for the "costal flexion" theory: the rider maintains the bend to the right, the torso is pushed to the left and the dorso-lumbar segment is bent very slightly to the right. The right haunch drops. But this is only a snapshot of half of the stride taken at the most favourable moment.

We can look at what happens next.

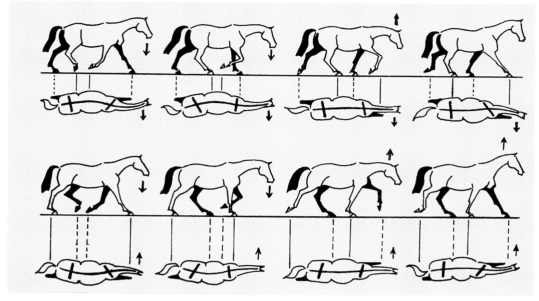

At walk

At trot

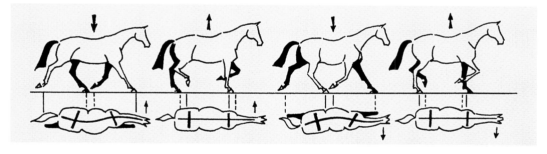

At canter

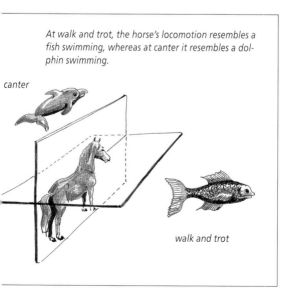

At walk and trot, the horse's locomotion resembles a fish swimming, whereas at canter it resembles a dolphin swimming.

canter

walk and trot

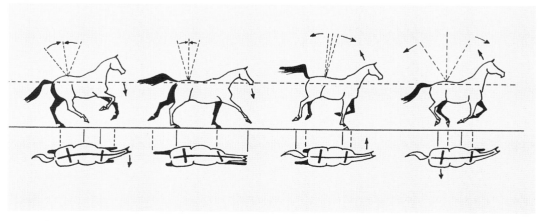

The undulations of the spine at walk, trot and canter (taken from "Reasoned Equitation" by Commandant Licart). For more clarity, the amplitude of the spine undulations have been deliberately exaggerated.

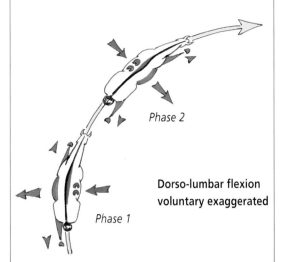

Phase 2

Dorso-lumbar flexion voluntary exaggerated

Phase 1

At trot, the horse's torso moves to the left or to the right according to the lateral pair which is closing or opening. During the first phase of the stride, the rider maintains the bend to the right and the dorso-lumbar segment also bends very slightly to the right. During the second phase of the stride, the spine forms an "S" shape: the neck bent to the right by the rider and the dorso-lumbar segment very slightly bent to the left.

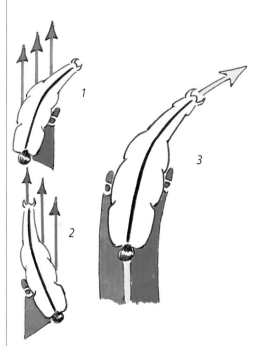

The rider's legs do not bend the horse. They channel the haunches to keep them exactly in line with the shoulders (3). This is only possible if the horse has learnt to distinguish between the inside and outside leg through careful education in the shoulder-in (1) and the travers (2)

2. The left diagonal pair is bearing weight and the right one is in flight: for fans of the "costal-flexion", everything is wrong since this time it is the left lateral pair which are closing and the right pair opening. The left haunch drops and the torso moves to the right. The horse is "S" shaped with its neck bent to the right by the rider and the dorso-lumbar segment is very slightly bent to the left.

> **Even when regularly repeated, no theory can overcome the imperious laws of locomotion. A horse cannot simultaneously move and maintain its spine in one position, whatever it is.**

In reality we can say this:

• Maintaining a distinct bend in the neck to the right favours dorso-lumbar flexion by a cumulative effect, whenever it occurs to the right.
• As opposed to this, it limits it, by subtraction, when it occurs to the left.

It is the bending of the neck that affects the movement of the back, and not the other way round; the claim that "costal flexion" imposed by the legs generates the bending of the neck has no basis. And yet this myth is held up as a principle.

This is one of the teachings of the official approach: "To bend your horse, ride it energetically and place your inside leg at the girth and your outside leg to the rear". This is combined with an increasing number of circles with strong legs in this position with the hope of bending the horse's body at the waist. Not only have we seen the vanity of this approach, but also the distinction between the inside and outside leg does not in theory exist for a young horse.

Until a horse has been schooled in shoulder-in, it does not know how to bring its hips in by moving in the opposite direction to the bend, under the action of the inside leg, placed by convention at the girth. Until the horse has been schooled in haunches-in, it does not know how to bring its haunches in by moving in the direction of the bend under the action of the outside leg, placed by convention behind the girth.

Without this careful education through elementary lateral work, the inside and outside leg have no meaning for a horse and have no effect that the rider can count on.

Conclusion

In movement, the facts show that the rider has strictly no power to maintain the bend in the horse's body with his own little legs. He should forget all such pretensions!

Whilst he can maintain the bend of the neck as he wants, for the rest he will use the inside leg when the horse tries to bring its haunches in to the inside, and the outside leg if it tries to move its haunches to the outside. It is as simple as that!

In other words, the rider's legs do not bend the horse, they channel the haunches to keep them exactly in line with the shoulders. This is quite an achievement in itself!

We could conclude that these are arguments which do not make much difference in the end. This is certainly true. An oasis is an oasis and a mirage is a mirage. If we obstinately consider the mirage to be an oasis it could have tragic consequences!

Convinced that they are doing the right thing, teachers and riders often try to use their legs and spurs to make their horse do something that nature did not intend.

Engagement of the hind legs

This leads to worry, contraction and continual harassment by the legs and the spurs… without any gain in forwards movement. By working hard for an illusion, the rider wastes his time and dulls his horse to the leg.

There is nothing to win in this game. The best thing is not to do it.

> The theory of the "costal-flexion" misjudges feelings and mistakes what we want for reality.
> This equestrian dogma is contrary to anatomical realities and essential requirements of locomotion.

· "Come on lad! No discussions – give me a costal flexion!"
· No chance!

Riders use a lot of legs and spurs to try and get their horse to do something that nature makes impossible. By working hard for an illusion the rider only manages to dull his horse to the legs.

Aiming to restore balance and achieve collection, dressage has a constant obsession with the "engagement of the hind legs in the direction of the centre of gravity".

This shortening of the weight-bearing base involves bringing the hind legs under the horse's mass and is meant to be achieved via demi-arrêts and transitions.

Engagement of the hind legs is asked for in transitions by the combined use of the seat, the legs and the hands.

> *"Releasing and acting on the reins is always done in conjunction with the appropriate weight and leg aids. For instance this is used in all half-halts and therefore in transitions between gaits or within a gait (lengthening and shortening the stride)."* (B1, page 65)
>
> *"Weighting the SEAT BONES requires the rider to hold his back more strongly."*
> *"This encourages the horse to increase the engagement of the hind legs under the horse's mass in the direction of the centre of gravity and to increase the weight that they bear."* (B1, page 60)
>
> *"Weighting both seat bones is used to increase the activity of the hind legs, in all halts, half-halts and in all transitions. In conjunction with propulsive legs, this weight aid encourages the two hind legs to advance in the direction of the centre of gravity and push more energetically."* (B1, page 59)

The simultaneous use of the weight, the hands and the legs for demi-arrêts – and therefore in all downward transitions? Just to be sure, we can start by analysing the expected effects of these aids, one by one.

Then we will move on to study the mechanism of transitions in terms of locomotion.

We will then see in what way the aforementioned aids can help improve balance through transitions.

The hand

We already know what to think of the famous "active hand". In fact it works by moving backwards. It does not balance, it acts as a brake and requires the support of propulsive aids to counter-act its unwanted effects.

If the hand moves backwards during a downward transition it does not rebalance the horse, it acts as a brake and puts the horse on its forehand. To improve balance during the transition, the rider must shift the horse's mass backwards by lifting the base of the neck.

From the dream...

... to the reality.

75kg (weight) + 25kg (pulling) = 100kg

"Weighting the seat bones" is only a reality if the rider clamps on to the saddle with all his strength by pulling on both reins!

If the rider sinks down on his two seat bones with all his weight on the back of a sensitive horse ridden bareback, he will not cause the active engagement of the hind legs. On the contrary, the horse will react by contracting its back muscles and consequently disengaging its hind legs.

The hand only objectively encourages the weight to shift backwards if it causes the base of the neck to rise. It is not enough to ask the horse to slow down to improve balance. Conversely we have to rebalance the horse to achieve a correct and useful transition.

The seat

Weighting the seat bones by holding the back would apparently cause the active engagement of the hind legs.

Weighting the seat bones? Whatever he does with his back, a rider who is already sitting and who weighs 75kg cannot claim to exert a pressure of 100kg on his seat bones – unless he manages to clamp himself into the saddle by pulling on both reins! (As he could do using the handles on a vaulting surcingle.) What we know about the "active hand" makes this plausible... but we would have to admit it!

So how does the seat act on the back? The rider's seat and the horse's back are separated by a saddle, a saddle pad and a saddle cloth. All of this is very well designed to isolate and protect one from the other. With this arrangement it is entirely an illusion that the seat bones have any effect whatsoever on the horse's back.

But never mind. We can take a horse, preferably with a sensitive skin and ride it bareback. The rider moves off at a walk and is careful to carry himself partly on his thighs. He then asks the horse to slow down and stop, by sitting as heavily as possible with both of his seat bones on his horse's back.

Result: the horse reacts by contracting its back muscles, hollows and consequently disengages its hind legs.

In summary, if weighting the seat bones has any effect, it is the opposite of that asserted by official theory.
Another dogma - the important thing is just to believe it, because an "engaging" seat does not exist.

The legs

To back up the supposed effects of the seat, "propulsive legs" are intended to increase the active engagement of the hind legs under the horse's mass. We can look at the technical and psychological aspects of the question within the context of schooling a young horse.

The psychology of impulsion

Dressage manuals limit themselves to a few general considerations and declarations of intent when it comes to animal psychology, but they do not refer to them at all in practice in this wealth of learning situations that we call dressage.

Whatever is being discussed, one expression comes back time and time again: "The horse must....". The horse "must" do nothing, as it is not a machine for producing dressage tests. It is dressage, in the noble sense of the word, which must be used to serve him, rather than the other way round.

By giving a "lesson of the leg" to his horse, the rider educates it to the impulsive meaning of the legs. By methodical conditioning, he has set up a reflex behaviour: pressure of the legs = forwards straight away!

However, there are two phases to the stride: engagement (with the limb in flight) and propulsion (with the limb bearing weight). On its own, "engagement" of the hind leg does not produce anything, it is when it "disengages" that it has a propulsive effect...and more particularly as the limb stretches out behind.

The rider has therefore taught his horse the following reflex action: pressure of the legs = active and immediate "disengagement" of the hind legs.

That this goes against the preconceived ideas in the official guidelines does not matter- it is an elementary and indisputable fact of locomotion.

> Legs = propulsion = extension of the hind legs.

Psychology and transitions

Analysing a "dressage" sequence.

In response to the rider's legs (whenever necessary backed up by a reminder by the whip)… the young horse moves into trot by the energetic extension of its hind legs… good lad!

A few seconds later, we slow him and return to walk, then halt using the same "propulsive legs"! The horse will firstly try to courageously and loyally move forward; but the "engaging" seat and the very, very "active" hands will be used to dissuade him, or even possibly to punish him! It has just understood, with a certain amount of anxiety that the legs no longer mean forwards! After a few seconds at halt, finally imposed with relative success,

we once again move off into trot! The rider closes his legs. Still under the impression of its recent misunderstanding the horse hesitates - and here the whip punishes him immediately! Poor horse! What is it meant to understand from all this inconsistency? Convinced that he is right and ready for a fight, the rider will make him give in to this disciplinary nonsense.

Unfortunately it is the horse's freshness and impulsion that will suffer from all these arbitrary aids as they oppose, cancel out and contradict.

The mechanism in transitions

Finally, we can take a look at exactly what happens in terms of this famous *"engagement of the hind legs towards the centre of gravity"* in transitions.

We could consult serious works on animal locomotion, but an attentive examination of photographs or slow motion films is enough to tell us what we need to know.

In terms of locomotion, we can initially distinguish two types of engagement:

• Alternate engagement of each hind leg: the longer the stride, the more one hind leg engages whilst the other propels (this at walk and trot).

· *"Okay for engaging! but active legs mean FORWARDS…Yes or No?"*
· *"What a bad lad! You've no respect for the rules!"*

If a driver wants, he can slow down by pressing the brake and the accelerator at the same time; but he should not then be surprised to find out that he's wearing out the brakes, wasting fuel, and that he regularly stalls, not to mention being considered a Sunday driver.

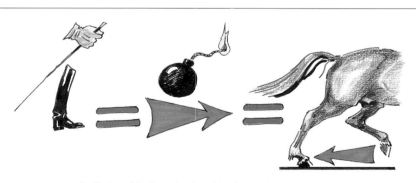

By methodical conditioning using the whip, the rider has taught the horse: "pressure of the legs = forward straight away!" However, to propel itself forward, the horse has to disengage its hind leg and stretch it out behind.

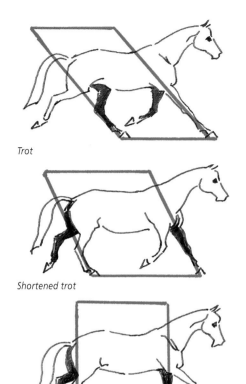

Trot

Shortened trot

Just before returning to walk

During the elementary transition from trot to walk *the horse starts by slowing its trot and reducing the length of stride until it reaches the speed of walk and transitions down to this gait. During this transition the diagonal pairs have remained strictly parallel: therefore the hind legs have not come further under the horse's body.*

(At canter, the limbs engage and disengage virtually simultaneously)

• The simultaneous engagement of the hind legs occurs through durable flexion of the lumbar back and the haunches and brings the limbs to work further under the horse's body – this is the engagement that we are interested in here.

• **Elementary level = studying the transition from trot to walk.**
The horse starts to slow its trot by reducing the length of stride, until it is at the speed of the walk and it then transitions down to this pace. During this transition the diagonal pair have remained strictly parallel. Therefore, not only have the hind legs not come further under the horse's body, but they have also reduced their alternate engagement during the whole slowing phase.

It is difficult to see how the legs and seat have the miraculous "engaging" virtues that they are supposed to have. They would have no reason to be involved in this transition.

People will object that things are different in collection. So let us have a look at that too.

• **Higher level = studying the transition from extended trot to passage.**
From extended trot to medium trot, then to so called "working trot", to "collected trot", to the "school trot" and lastly to a "gentle passage" and to a "full passage". The horse maintains its activity (the difference with the previous case). The movement of the legs becomes more elevated as it reduces in length of stride. The initially extreme "over-tracking" of the extended trot is gradually reduced. Lastly in passage the horse "under-tracks".

From one end to the other of this transition the diagonal pairs in the weight-bearing phase have remained parallel. Not only do horses not increase the engagement of the hind legs to reach passage, but also the most expressive horses in this air execute it by extending their weight-bearing base to the rear. This means that, even during transitions leading to a high level of collection, not only is there no simultaneous advancing of the hind legs under the horse's body, but also their alternating engagement reduces with the shortening of the strides!

If the legs are involved at all, it is to tell the horse that there should be no loss of activity with the shortening of the gait, but under no circumstances to cause an illusion of engagement of the hind legs.

Overview: due to the horse's locomotion, the simultaneous engagement of the hind legs requires the constant flexion of the haunches, which is incompatible with the extension movement needed for forwards movement.

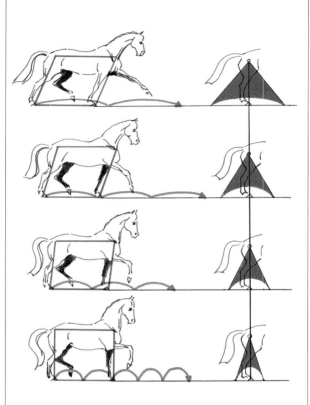

During the transition from extended trot to the so called "working trot", to "collected trot" and lastly to passage, the diagonal pairs that are weight-bearing have remained parallel. The alternate engagement of the hind legs reduces with the shortening of the stride. This means that even during transitions to a high level of collection, the hind legs do not move further under the horse's body.

During a transition leading to a high level of collection, the horse does not shorten its diagonal weight-bearing base: from extended trot...

...to collected trot, the diagonal pairs have remained parallel.
Horses with the most expressive passages often produce this air by lengthening their base to the rear.
Photos: Laurioux

Expressive passages

By Egon von Neindorff
Ernst Lindenbauer, Nuno Oliveira,
Joao Trigueros d'Aragao,
Richard Wätjen and Colonel Wattel
(from top left to bottom right) show
that horses do not shorten their
weight-bearing base in this highly
collected air – rather the contrary.

In fact, the hind legs only really come further towards the centre of gravity in extreme collection:

• in a canter that is virtually on the spot (pirouettes and terre à terre)…
• in collected halts (the so called parade by past masters)…
• in a piaffe worthy of the name, and in the pesade.

*The horse also shows **increased flexion of the haunches in the "parade"** or in other words a collected halt,…*

Locomotion clearly shows: *the hind legs only really come further towards the centre of gravity in extreme collection, for example in a canter that is virtually on the spot for the pirouette.*

…in a true piaffe…

… and in the pesade. Photos: Laurioux

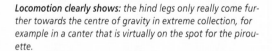

Conclusion

Official dressage consistently gives mechanistic and quantitative concepts to equitation. It shouts: "Forwards! Forwards!" Which is indisputable. But it considers impulsion as due. It describes what the horse "must" do, but explains nothing about how to educate it to the legs.

In the end it limits itself to recommending "stronger aids" when the horse does not respond in a satisfactory manner, and stresses:

"Please note. Many riders tend use too much hand and not enough legs and seat. This tendency must be firmly fought."
(B1, page 67)
(F N Rictlinien für Reiten und Fahren, Band 1, seite 80)

The correct use of the aids above all depends on their nature rather than their intensity. Something that is correct but too strong simply needs to be revised downwards – whereas something that is incorrect, whether it is strong or not, should simply be got rid of. Making stronger use of the aids, even if this is the seat and the legs, cannot be a goal in itself.

Dressage is "correct" in every sense of the term when it tends towards using fewer and fewer aids – when, according to La Guérinière it preserves the horse's "will to go", or when according to Baucher, it provides impulsion with a *descente de jambes*.

> Firmly believing in the utopian approaches of "costal flexion" and "engagement of the hind legs", riders desensitise their horses to their legs for no reason and therefore dull and damage the very motor of equitation: impulsion.

In summary

• Flexion of the poll by pushing with the legs on fixed and low hands that resist = active legs without any increase in forwards movement!
• Legs acting to bend the horse around the inside leg = illusion, and active legs without any gain in movement!
• Demi-arrêts and transitions using the legs to engage the hind legs under the horse's body = chasing rainbows, and active legs associated with a reduction in forwards movement!
• Halts and rein-backs, still with the support of propulsive aids = active legs to reach a neutral point and to reverse the forwards movement!

All in all the rider uses his legs much more often to contain, reduce or cancel forwards movement than to produce it. This leads to the use of spurs, whips and assistance from the ground when needing to train piaffe.

This gives a muscular and laborious style of riding, working the horse by force and by compression. There is no surprise that these concepts require the selection of outstanding horses in terms of aptitude and goodwill. It is the only way to have a small chance of overcoming these "difficulties".

If the seat and the legs had the virtues that conventional dressage associates with them, we would see horses, even modest horses, showing genuine collection. However, we mainly see exceptional horses with poor, and even imitation piaffes.

> Anatomical realities, the basic requirements of locomotion and the demands of psychology all favour the separate and moderate use of the aids. All of which confirms the words of the last teachings of F. Baucher: "Hand without legs, legs without hand".

Finally, we can note that with his incomparable blend of common sense and finesse, La Guérinière made no mention of any theories on the "costal flexion" or the "engaging" power of the seat – yet another area in which official dressage should give up its claim to this Master!

Well-bred horse and stifling rider: low hands and lots of legs!

THE SEAT

Moving around with a child on your shoulders gives an impression of your own impact on the horse.

A rider with a good seat, in other words one that allows him to move smoothly with the horse, can use this as an aid. This "seat aid" or "weight aid", is in fact an aid of balance.

The horse feels variations in the rider's balance just as we can feel those of a child sitting on our shoulders.

If you weigh 75kg and you move around with a child weighing 12 to 13kg on your shoulders you will have an impression of your own impact when you ride a horse of around 450kg - it is considerable!

We will look at two aspects of training in which the role of the seat aids is particularly important: lateral work and canter.

Lateral work

"In all lateral movements the rider must sit to the inside with more weight on the inside seat-bone."
"Incorrect distribution of the rider's weight disturbs the horse's balance and rhythm." (FN Guidelines for Riding and Driving, German Equestrian Federation, vol. 2, page 37.)

We can look at a lateral work sequence just taken at random for the purposes of this exercise:

- Circle to the right...
- Shoulder-in to the right...
- Half-pass to the right...
- Counter shoulder-in to the right on the curve...
- Renvers along the wall...

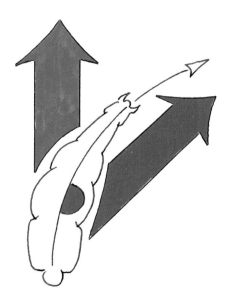

For shoulder-in, the dressage manuals recommend that the rider weights the inside seat-bone.

- Renvers on the curve.

We can see that if the rider wants to keep his seat to the side of the bend, he must always sit on the right. However, the horse frequently changes direction (six times), crossing its legs either to the right or to the left. The second principle means that the rider should adapt his seat every time – but the first principle forbids it. This is a major problem, the rider is acting wrongly half of the time. There is not even consistency in the error (the seat on the opposite side to the movement all the time) which would at least give the horse something to understand!

All in all, the two above-mentioned points prove absolutely incompatible.

Case study: the shoulder-in

For this, one of the most classical of all exercises, official dressage recommends that the rider sits to the inside. Two experiments can clarify this.

Experiment 1

Take a large ball, as used in the circus. Place it along the wall. Stand on it and face inwards at an angle of 30° from the wall (shoulder-in) on the right rein.

If you actually manage to move along the wall on the ball by weighting your right leg, (i.e. weight to the left) you will have produced a phenomenon that would be of interest to scientists and that many circuses would certainly be ready to pay a lot of money for as part of their show!

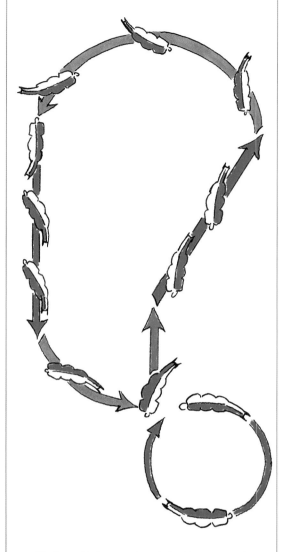

The laws of balance are formal: the rider must use the weight of his seat (in red) according to the direction in which the horse is moving, even if the bend remains the same throughout the lateral work sequence. Here for example volte to the right, shoulder-in to the right, half-pass to the right, counter shoulder-in to the right on the curve, renvers along the wall, renvers on the curve.

Experiment 2

Bring two candidates into your riding school.

Ask the smallest to sit on the shoulders of the strongest. Place them on the track. On the right rein, facing 30° from the wall.

Give your instructions: "Mr Horse, you have to move according to the changes in your rider's balance to keep him upright on your shoulders as well as possible."

If you ask the "rider" to lean to the right, the "horse" will move to the right. He will definitely not move to the left, along the wall. How disappointing!

But you can persist: take the "rider" to one side and ask him to persevere. Ask him to pull the head of his "horse" backwards and energetically encourage him forward with his right heel in his sides whilst continuing to lean to the right. Of course, they may not speak to each other afterwards!

The "rider" will accuse his horse of being unwilling. The "horse" will defend himself and point out the inconsistent and arbitrary demands of its rider. But if the "horse" is basically a nice guy, he will end up giving in to this unnatural and tiring situation. You can now be happy - this will confirm your theory. But you will be the only one who is pleased!

It is often possible to impose just about anything on a horse, even if it is complete nonsense. But by doing so we abuse its goodwill and limit its resources. We must remember that riding can only be classical, in the noble sense of the term, if it respects nature.

Balance before bend:
In shoulder in, the horse moves to its outside, the rider must therefore sit on the outside to remain harmonious with the horse's balance. A circus artist who moves a large ball along the track would do the same.

Phase 1:
Left diagonal pair flight phase Engagement of the right hind

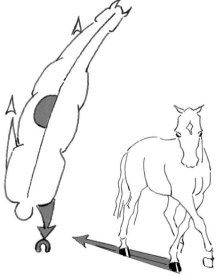

Phase 2:
Left diagonal pair weight-bearing phase Propulsion of the right hind leg

Shoulder-in to the right in trot: during the flight phase of the left diagonal pair (phase 1), the rider can support the activity of the right hind leg with his inside leg. During phase 2, the right hind pushes in the direction of the left shoulder. The rider weights his seat to the left to encourage and accompany the lateral movement to the left.

What is the rational way to use the seat in shoulder-in?

Shoulder-in to the right in trot

The horse moves along the line of its left diagonal pair, and we can distinguish two phases:

• Flight of the left diagonal pair:
engagement of the right hind lowering the right haunch and the right side of the horse's back.
The rider's right hip drops and this is the point where his inside leg may possibly support the oblique engagement of the right hind.
• Weight-bearing of the left diagonal pair:

This is the propulsion phase: the right hind leg pushes in the direction of the left shoulder. The right haunch rises whilst the left one and the left side of the back drops. During this phase, the rider's left hip drops, and this is the right time to weight the seat to encourage and accompany the lateral movement to the left.

> Simple, consistent and natural aids make the shoulder-in a remarkable key to progress which can be used right from the start of training.

The two phases of the shoulder-in to the right: during the flight phase of the left diagonal pair, the right hind leg engages.

During the weight-bearing phase of the left diagonal pair, the right hind leg pushes.
Photos: Slawik

Various lateral work exercises

We can look at the features of the main lateral exercises in terms of locomotion, balance and therefore the use of the rider's seat. With a right bend:

1. Shoulder-in on the circle
The horse turns to the right by pivoting around its right foreleg at every stride. It therefore balances itself towards the inside shoulder - seat to the right.

This is the most natural position to teach the horse to yield its haunches and to move away from the leg.

2. Shoulder-in and counter shoulder-in on the straight line
The horse moves towards its left shoulder, with the wall to the rear or to the front - seat to the left.

This position is used to straighten the horse and to approach collected work.

Shoulder-in on a straight line: the horse moves along the line of its left diagonal pair: seat to the left.

The same is true for the counter shoulder-in: seat to the outside.
Photos: Laurioux

In the shoulder-in on the circle, the rider sits to the inside because the horse turns by pivoting around its inside foreleg at every stride.

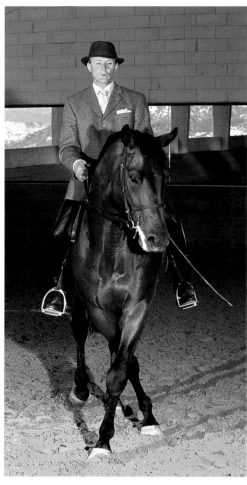

In the counter shoulder-in on the circle to the left, the horse crosses its forelegs to the right and pivots around its right hind at every stride. The rider sits to the right.

In the travers on the circle to the right. The horse turns right by pivoting around its right hind. The rider therefore sits to the right.

Renvers on the circle to the left, the horse turns to the left by pivoting around its left shoulder. The rider sits to the left. Photos: Laurioux

3. Counter shoulder-in on the circle

The horse turns to the left by pivoting around its left hind on every stride. It therefore balances around its outside hind- seat to the left.

This position lightens the shoulders and helps encourage the crossing of the forelegs.

4. Travers on the circle

The horse turns to the right and pivots around its right hind. It therefore weights its inside hind - seat to the right.

This position is useful to develop the crossing of the forelegs and collection.

5. Renvers on the circle

The horse turns to the left and pivots around its left shoulder. It therefore weights its outside shoulder- seat to the left.

This position develops the crossing of the hind legs.

Whether in travers, renvers or half-pass, the horse is moving along the line of its right diagonal pair. The rider therefore sits to the right. Photos: Laurioux

6. Travers, renvers and half-pass

When executed on the straight line, these three exercises involve the horse making the same movement. The only things that change are the lines on which they are executed: travers and renvers along the wall and half-pass on an oblique line.

The horse always moves in the direction of its bend in these three positions - seat to the right.

In half-pass, the horse moves in the direction of the bend: at trot...

... and at canter. Photos: Slawik

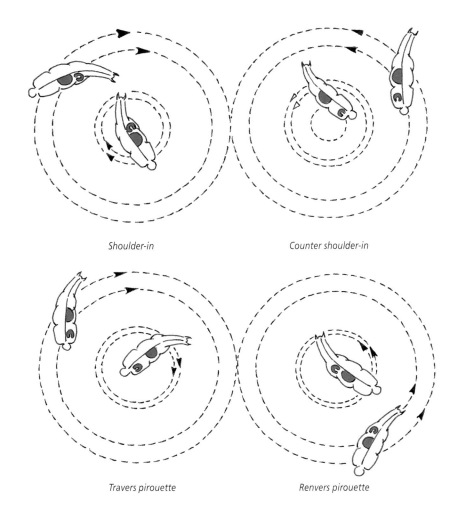

Shoulder-in

Counter shoulder-in

Travers pirouette

Renvers pirouette

Overview of lateral exercises on the circle: these exercises allow the rider to balance his horse more over one limb or the other and to develop lateral mobility of the shoulders or the haunches.

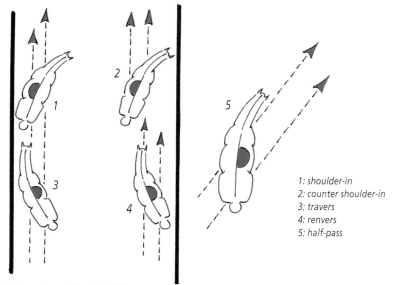

1: shoulder-in
2: counter shoulder-in
3: travers
4: renvers
5: half-pass

Overview of lateral exercises on the straight line:
Independently of the bend, the rider always puts his weight in the direction of movement (shown in red).

These exercises provide the rider with a virtually unlimited range of strategies. They allow him to accurately target gymnastic exercises for the horse according to its problems and needs in terms of balance and locomotion. They allow him to find fundamental solutions to a large number of problems and to infinitely vary the work carried out.

They are therefore very important. As long as inconsistent seat aids do not muddle the horsewith pointless and insurmountable complications.

Overview

Due to the universal laws of gravity and the balance of two bodies, one on top of the other, the rider's centre of gravity must move in the direction of the movement that he wants from the horse. Bend of the neck has nothing to do with it and costal flexion even less so, since it is simply an illusion.

Riders often create difficulties for the horse in lateral work by wrongly believing that they can hold the horse in an overall bend by weighting the inside seat-bone. Although it is meant to be the most important of all aids, in many cases the seat will then become a handicap for the horse.

These problems have two types of consequences:

• Due to the frequent problems that result from contradictions between the hands, the legs and the seat, dressage reduces lateral work to the strict minimum corresponding to the exercise required in the dressage test. Consequently it dumbs down its approach, singularly limits the horse's gymnastic programme, restricts itself to stereotyped, dull work and deprives itself of gentle and incredibly effective solutions, especially for mediocre or difficult subjects.

• We commonly hear leading sports dressage personalities learnedly claiming that shoulder-in is the most difficult lateral movement. Do we need to remind the competition dressage world that it claims its heritage from La Guérinière? To quote the father of the shoulder-in:

"This lesson produces so many good effects at once, that I keep it as the first and the last of all those that you can give to the horse, to make it become totally supple and give perfect freedom to every part of it."

The last lesson because it remains the key to straightness and collection throughout training. The first lesson because it is the most natural and therefore the easiest position.

Indeed every time a horse moves to the side by itself (moving around something it is scared of, avoiding a bull charge in the bullring or running out at a jump at the last minute), it always does this by bending its neck in the opposite direction to the direction of movement. We can remember (natural crookedness) that the bend favours the weighting of the outside shoulder and therefore movement in this direction.

While La Guérinière did not say anything about the role of the seat in the shoulder-in, this is probably because he did not think it useful to state the obvious. It is not the shoulder-in that is so difficult, it is illogical and contradictory aids that make it such a feat.

This is how shoulder-in has changed from its classical role as a gentle and irreplaceable solution at all stages of training, and been given a technocratic status as a difficult movement, almost a new air!

Modern dressage most often only uses it symbolically or as an "imitation" whilst at the same time fully embracing all the delights of a useless fad: the "leg yield".

The "leg yield" has today taken over from the shoulder-in as the exercise used to start lateral work, to train horses and educate rid-

When a horse moves to the side by itself, for instance to avoid an object that it fears, it always does so by bending its neck in the opposite direction to its movement: in other words in a shoulder-in.

ers. By definition the first learning exercise must be the most easy and be useful.

So we can see how "leg yielding" measures up:

• The horse learns to do lateral work with slight lateral flexion limited to the poll and no bend in the neck.
At this stage, it would certainly take quite a rider to be able to control the poll with such precision. It is the bending of the neck which causes a natural shifting of the weight to the shoulder which must start the movement to the side. This is also what causes opposition of the shoulder with the inside hind and encourages the lateral movement of the hindquarters. The shoulder-in is therefore more natural and easy.
• The stated virtues of the "leg yield" are that it supples and relaxes.

What suppling exercises can claim to work without bending the horse? This exercise flatters a lack of desire or an inability to bend the neck and is limited to a rather laborious control of stiffness.

• The rules describe the respective roles of the inside and outside leg. Applied to an un-bent

horse, this has no sense. And here we are suddenly playing down the importance of the famous "costal flexion", which is actually an illusion, but which is supposed to be understood beforehand on simple curves.
• The seat must be put to the so-called "inside". This is another aberration in terms of balance, as seen in the shoulder-in: the seat is weighted on the opposite side to the movement.
• The recommended angle is between 35° and 45° at most.

This is really excessive for a careful initiation to lateral work (remember that an extreme for half-pass is around 45° and this is considered as being of the greatest difficulty).

• *"The exercise is generally carried out at walk, although for more advanced riders on the appropriate horses it can be ridden in working trot."* (FN Guidelines for Riding and Driving, German Equestrian Federation, *vol. 1, page 95.*)

This is easy to understand considering its senseless difficulty.

Overall, the "leg yield" (strange terminology in fact: when is a horse authorised not to yield to the leg?) combines so many inconsistencies and pointless difficulties that it is a problem rather than a solution. It is a pure technocratic product, without any practical justification and without any link to classical equitation, a "new air" that has to be drilled into the horse in order to present it to examination officials and judges that want to see it.

Knowing all the benefits of the shoulder-in (the most natural position): suppling, straightening, balancing and collecting, we can understand why La Guérinière did not invent the "leg yield". Forgetting it and instead focusing on correctly understanding the shoulder-in would therefore save time and be more effective.

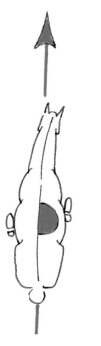

The manuals recommend that the rider weights the inside seat bone for a canter strike-off, here to the right.

Canter strike-off

The manuals recommend that the rider weights his inside seat-bone. Therefore sitting to the right to canter on the right leg.

A reminder of aspects of the natural crookedness of the horse and its effects: a horse naturally bent to the right is more willing and finds it easier to canter on the right leg. Horses that are very crooked will sometimes totally refuse to canter on the left leg.

However, we know that a horse that is naturally bent to the right will weight its left shoulder and swings its haunches to the right.

Initially it would therefore appear that weighting the outside lateral pair would help the canter strike-off.

"The diagrams produced by Marey using his recording device have shown that in a right lead canter, it is the left lateral pair that bears the most weight and that consequently does the most work (weight-bearing by the left hind, receiving the propulsion of the right hind on the left foreleg). This explains why a horse which has a problem in a right limb is more willing to canter to the right." (Licart, *Reasoned Equitation*)

Information taken from Extracts of Reports to the Academy of Science by Marey, 1887.

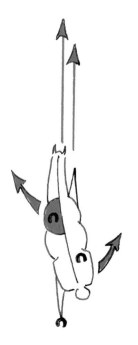

A horse naturally bent to the right will always be more willing and able to canter on the right leg. Its natural bend to the right will lead it to weight its left shoulder and swing its haunches in to the right.

Two types of canter strike-off:
at the top, the horse canters to the right by anticipating the weight-bearing of the right foreleg. The right shoulder is weighted, the canter starts by lifting the croup. This type of strike-off is favoured by weighting the seat to the right. At the bottom: canter strike-off by anticipating weight-bearing of the left hind leg. The left hind leg is weighted, the canter starts by lifting the shoulders. This type of strike-off is favoured by weighting the seat to the left.

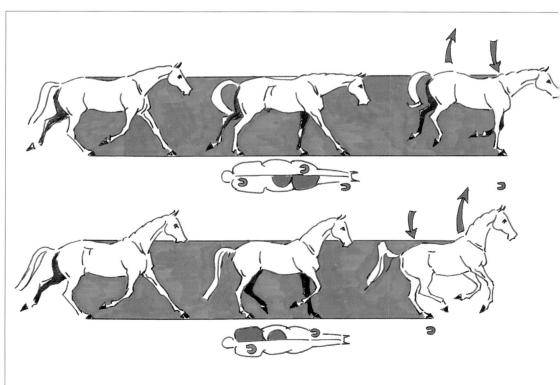

Confirmation by experience.

To understand locomotion, it is useful to simulate the gaits, just like children do. Put a few small stones in one of your shoes, for instance the right one. And now canter!

Without fail you will simulate canter to the right because this is the only mechanism that allows you to relieve weight-bearing on the right foot and take most of your weight on the left leg. Anyone who continues to doggedly canter to the left could be considered a masochist.

Two types of canter strike-off

Slow motion films show that canter strike-offs can take place according to two different mechanisms:

Canter strike off to the right from trot:

• By anticipating weight-bearing of the right foreleg. This type of strike-off is often called: "by loss of balance". In fact it starts by anticipating the weight-bearing of the right foreleg and lifting the croup.
• By anticipating the weight-bearing of the left hind. This strike-off is so-called "by gain of balance", since it starts by the anticipated weight-bearing of the left hind leg and the lifting of the shoulders.

Overall, we can see that a canter strike-off to the right occurs by dissociation of the right diagonal... and this is:

• either by anticipating weight-bearing of the right foreleg - an option that is naturally favoured by weighting the right side of the seat.
• or by anticipating weight-bearing of the left hind leg - an option favoured by weighting the left side of the seat.

If you carry a heavy case with your left hand, you will easily be able to simulate canter to the right, whereas canter to the left will be much more difficult.

N.B.: Canter strike-off never starts by engaging the inside hind, a common misconception. However, at the point where the inside hind leg reaches under the horse's body, the horse's back drops on this side and the rider does sit more to the inside. However this corresponds to the second phase of the stride. The canter is already underway. Naturally the canter strike-off aids must act before the horse does this.

Confirmation by experience

Take a heavy suitcase, carry it in your left hand and simulate canter strike-offs:

• To the left: the weight of the suitcase will tend to move you to the left and hinder the movement of your left leg. You will be uncomfortable and will have to compensate for this imbalance with a large amount of effort, notably from the back.
• On the right leg: you will balance the weight of the case by bearing a lot of weight on your left leg. This will automatically free up your right leg which will find it easy to start cantering. You can limit your effort by making it as efficient as possible.

> Canter tends to occur on the leg opposite to the weighted lateral pair. This ties in with the requirements of animal locomotion: "The principle of minimum effort".

"All combinations of aids that slow down the movement of the left lateral pair, lightening the right lateral pair and enhancing its forwards movement are suitable to influence canter strike-off to the right."
(Commandant Licart, Reasoned Equitation)

Strategy for teaching canter strike-offs

Moving on from looking at the balance that is most favourable to cantering and the canter strike-off mechanism, we can determine various learning approaches.

The basic strike-off

With horses that are very crooked, it is advisable to achieve as many successful strike-offs as possible on the difficult leg (e.g. to the left for a horse that is naturally bent to the right). This is done by giving the horse the necessary basics - shoulder-in and travers.

Ask for canter strike-offs to the left from travers to the left along the wall. Hold the haunches with the right leg then weight the seat to the right and close the left leg at the girth to give canter.

The travers places the left lateral pair in front of the right one, which favours the advancing of the left hind leg and the pushing of the right hind leg. The bend to the left stops the horse falling onto the left shoulder by weighting the right one. All of these aspects imply a strike-off to the left. Steinbrecht expresses this very clearly by designating the travers as "the position for canter".

The strike-off by "gain of balance"

Looking at canter strike-offs, for example on the left leg, any situation which weights the right lateral pair and relieves weight to the left lateral pair will be favourable.

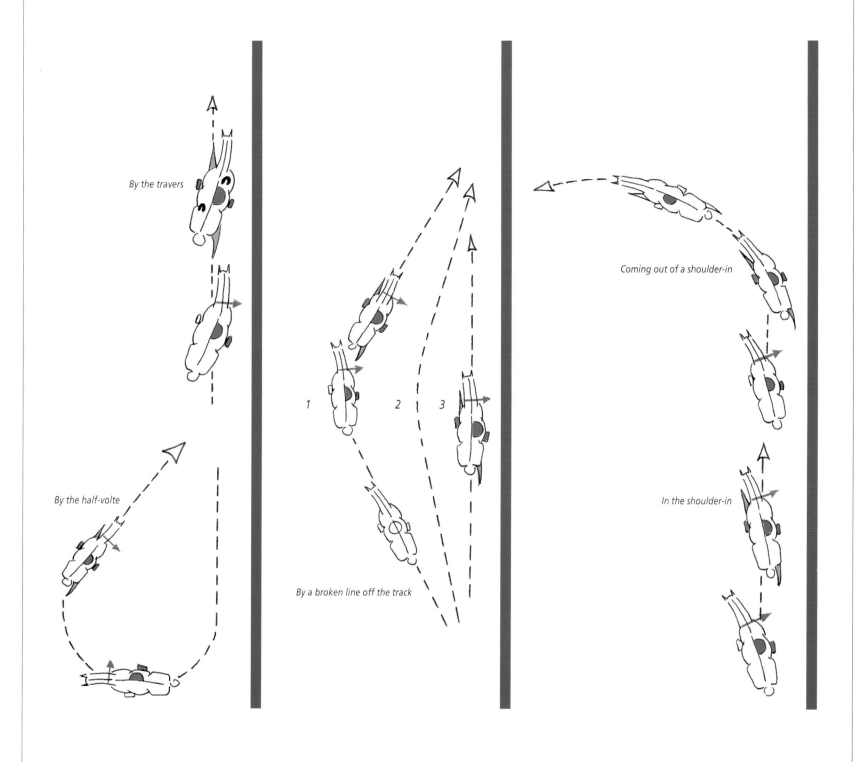

By the travers

By the half-volte

1   2   3

By a broken line off the track

Coming out of a shoulder-in

In the shoulder-in

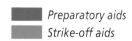 Preparatory aids

Strike-off aids

Exercises to teach a canter strike-off to the left:
On the left: the rider will obtain a basic strike-off by asking for it in a travers, then on a half-volte.
In the middle: to teach the horse the canter strike-off on the straight line, the rider does a broken line off the track and back again (1), gradually reducing the size (2) until he progressively gets a strike-off on the straight line (3).
On the right: the rider works on the straightness and collection of canter strike-offs by cantering after a shoulder-in with the horse striking off on an oblique line or on a large circle. Then he will be able to ask the horse to canter whilst remaining in the shoulder-in.

To achieve this balance, nothing is as effective or as simple as turning in a counter-bend using a neck-rein on the left.

• For a canter strike-off to the left using a half-volte, starting on the right rein: half-circle in counter-bend using a left neck-rein and seat weighted to the right. The right leg is slightly back, holding the haunches. At the tangent between the curve and the oblique line, action of the left leg: canter.
• For a canter strike-off to the left by a broken line off of the track: on the left rein, leave the long side on an oblique line and maintain the bend to the left. To go back to the track, turn to the right using a left neck-rein and weight the seat on the right, with the right leg back to hold the haunches. When the horse starts the second oblique line, act with the left leg at the girth: canter.

By reducing the amount that you come off of the track, this approach will gradually lead to a canter strike-off on a straight line. In the end, the same aids will cause a strike-off to the left without leaving the track.

Canter strike-offs with a focus on straightness and collection

Due to its mechanism, canter contains a potential tendency for the haunches to swing in. Specific work will ensure absolute straightness in canter strike-offs.

• Canter strike-off to the left following a shoulder-in to the left: shoulder-in to the left along the long side (seat already to the right). Keep sitting to the right, contain the movement of the haunches by putting the right leg back, then action of the left leg at the girth: the horse starts to canter by moving off on an oblique line or on a large circle. Preparation for the next stage.

• Strike-off in shoulder-in: place the horse in a slight shoulder-in to the left along the wall and canter whilst remaining in this posture. The shoulder-in position hinders the canter mechanism but has the advantage of cancelling out any swinging-in of the haunches as well as collecting the gait.

Overview

More than many other exercises, the canter strike-off is based on a linguistic code set up by training. Empirical riders, always against any analysis or justification of their procedures, will avoid the question with the following unshakeable argument: "The main thing is that it works!" Naturally, with a few tricks and quite a lot of cleverness, we could even school a horse to strike off to canter on the left when we pull its right ear. What a great circus trick!

But this does not mean that all approaches have the same value. To comply with the realities of locomotion and the requirements of balance, canter strike-offs require the rider to weight his seat to the outside. Following this we will see that the unnatural choice of weighting the seat to the inside for the canter strike-off (sufficient with gifted horses, but not with the others) leads to serious and sometimes insurmountable difficulties when approaching counter-canter and flying changes.

In any case, the real test in this respect, involves a lot more than successfully doing tempi changes with a gifted horse. It is about giving a good counter-canter and correct flying changes to any horse.

And in this respect, if the rider does not get to the heart of the problem, he has very little chance of success.

Counter-Canter

Official instructions

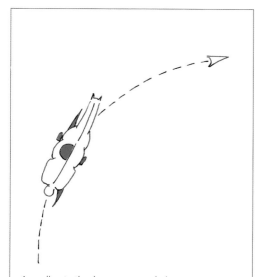

According to the dressage manuals, in counter-canter the rider must bend his horse to the outside and also weight his seat to the outside.

We can make two observations: we are missing any progression intended to bring the horse to be able to do counter-canter and we are also missing any reference to problem situations and ways of remedying them. Once again we only deal with the hypothesis of quite a gifted horse in order to get through the test without a problem.

We can review all this with a precise example: a horse that is naturally bent to the right, and with a distinct preference for cantering on the right leg, that we bring to counter-canter on the left leg, for the first time. Since it is on the left leg the rider changes rein and tries to go around the corner whilst maintaining the initial canter.

By doing this he rides his horse on a curve to the right, on a left canter lead with the following aids:

- Right leg back and left leg at the girth…
- Neck bent to the left…
- Seat weighted to the left.

Result: faced with a new problem and unprepared, the horse is worried and tense. We should do everything to make its job easier. But:

- The corner to the right would require the seat to be weighted to the right. Here, it is to the left in order to maintain the regulatory aids for the canter strike-off to the left.
- Having to stay on a left-lead canter on a curve to the right, the horse really needs to be able to freely advance its left shoulder instead of the right one. But the bend to the left restricts its movement and shortens it.
- Associated with the right leg back, the bend to the left encourages the horse to move its hips to the left and to fall on the right shoulder.

Under these conditions the counter-canter generally results in either the horse disuniting regularly in front (it would be considered

to have "poor balance"!) or, if it is gifted enough to do this, the exercise produces a short canter, often with the hips out.

This approach to counter-canter is of no interest. It is a pointless difficulty that has been dictated as a dressage ritual, and the best thing would be to avoid doing it. Show jumping riders do not bother with it and they do very well.

A useful approach to counter-canter

Look for optimum conditions of locomotion and balance to enable the horse to perform correctly.

Locomotion

When cantering freely, the horse bends the neck to the side opposite its canter lead on every stride: e.g.: when cantering to the left, it only bends its neck to the right, forming a series of "S" shapes on every stride.

This movement helps the horse move the left shoulder in front of the right one. It is therefore reasonable to think that in a difficult situation, in which the horse must stay on the left leg, the helpful bend will naturally be a bend to the right.

Training considerations
- Circle to the left. When the rider works in the left canter on a circle to the left, he is meant to maintain the bend to the left. This avoids the horse falling on the left shoulder and restricts the movement of the left foreleg which is on the inside track (shorter strides).
- Circle to the right. But when the rider changes rein, the left shoulder must not only remain in front of the right one to maintain the left canter, it must also produce longer strides since it is on an outside track.

Disunited canter in front

Short canter with the hips out

If the rider rides his horse in counter-canter with the bend to the outside and weights his seat to the same side, he encourages it to disunite in front or shorten its stride and put its hips out.

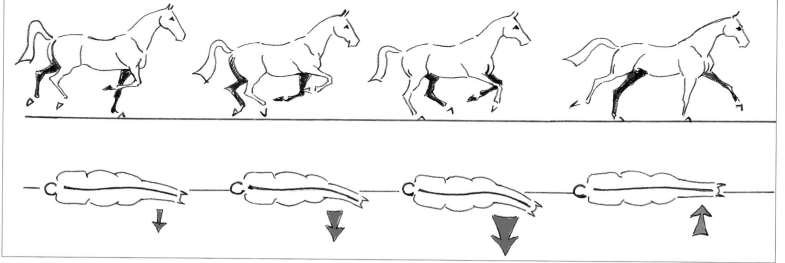

At a free canter the horse bends its neck at every stride on the opposite side to the leg that it is cantering on, for example to the right for a left canter. (Movements of the spine deliberately exaggerated.)

The horse therefore needs a position which contains the gesture of the right shoulder and amplifies that of the left. These conditions are naturally combined by bending the neck to the right (mastoido-humeral muscles on the left side are stretched).

Balance

The curve to the right implies that the centre of gravity is brought to the right and therefore the rider sits to the right. But this balancing aid must be in line with the use of the seat that helps maintain the left canter. Therefore it is obvious that it is only by weighting the seat to the outside in the canter strike-off that we will be consistent with the laws of balance when it comes to counter-canter. One confirms the other.

Straightness

Bending to the right allows us to limit the loading of the right shoulder and by using a neck-rein we shift the forehand to the left therefore bringing it in front of the haunches (which always tend to escape). This confirms the correct basis of only straightening using the hand (as seen in the first chapter).

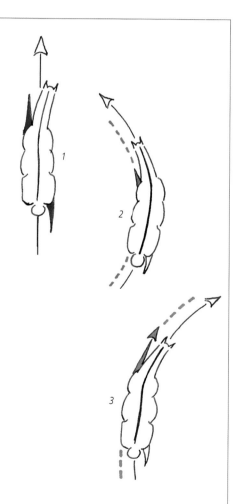

Consequences of the bend on the movement of the front legs at canter

For a left canter the horse naturally tends to bend the neck to the right (1). By bending the neck to the left the rider restricts the movement of the left foreleg (2). By bending the neck to the right, he amplifies the movement of the left foreleg (3).

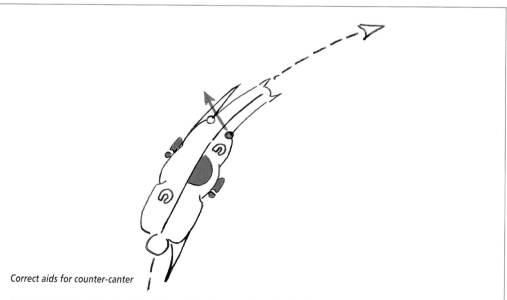

Correct aids for counter-canter

For counter-canter to the right, the rider weights his seat to the right, bends the horse to the inside and if necessary shifts the forehand to the left in front of the haunches using a neck-rein on the right.

In fact, any attempt to do this using the legs would lead to the canter disuniting or to the horse changing leg.

With these conditions of position and balance, counter-canter can be executed by any horse and any rider. Particularly if a well-thought-out progression carefully prepares them for this.

1. Counter-bend in canter

Get the horse used to changing bend. For example: on a circle to the left on the left lead, put the horse in a bend to the right. Turn in the counter-bend by using an outside neck-rein, in canter, as in walk and trot.

2. Counter-canter without changing rein

On the left rein, with a left canter, broken line off of the track as follows:

- Bend to the left to leave the track.
- Change the bend on the first part of the broken line.
- Turn right with the bend to the right (seat to the right to come back on the second part of the broken line).
- Bend to the left to go back to the track.
- Gradually increase the amount that you leave the track. The rider quickly manages to do a broken line to the centre line.

3. Counter-canter from a half-volte

- At the end of the long side, do a small half-volte to the left in a counter-bend.
- Maintain the bend to the right along the long side.
Go around the first corner making it as shallow as possible. Return to walk and rest.
- If the horse remains relaxed we can then go around two corners... and lastly continue on a large full circle.

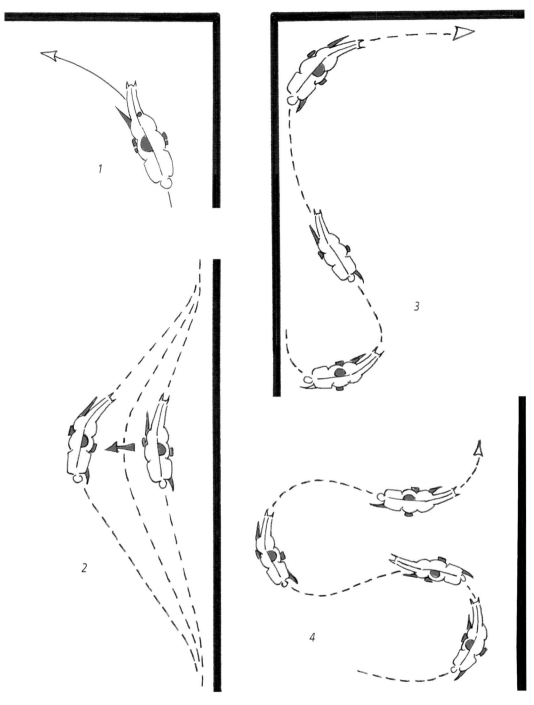

List of exercises to teach counter-canter
1: The rider gets the horse used to changing bend in canter.
2: He then does a slight broken line off the track and gradually increases the amplitude of this until the horse does a large broken line off the track to the centre of the school and back.
3: Following this preparation he can ask the horse to change the rein using a half-volte and go around the next corner in counter-canter.
4: When the horse becomes familiar with the counter-canter it will have no problem performing other figures if the rider is careful to establish the counter-bend for a few strides before going into a new curve in counter-canter.

Analysing locomotion confirms that counter-cantering with the neck bent to the inside is correct.

This approach gives more amplitude to the counter-canter stride. Photos: Laurioux

4. Figure of eight and serpentine

These figures pose no problem to horses if the rider is careful to give a counter-bend a few strides before going into a new curve in counter-canter.

Overview

Counter-canter must be ridden with the neck bent to the inside. This frees up the movement of the shoulders, gives amplitude to the canter stride and re-establishes straightness. Counter-canter unequivocally confirms the correctness of weighting the seat to the outside for canter strike-offs.

By analysing counter-canter we can see that putting the weight to the same side as the canter lead is a rigid, unjustified dogma that handicaps the horse.

In dressage tests, it would be a good idea to judge the counter-canter on its amplitude and therefore to have it with a distinct bend to the inside rather than focusing on the regulatory bend to the outside which shortens the stride and deprives many horses of this useful exercise.

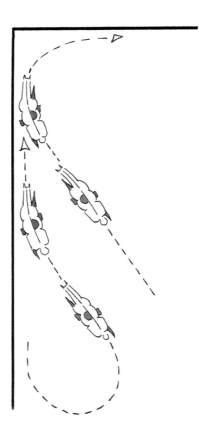

Dressage manuals recommend that riders teach the flying change by having the horse change to the inside when changing direction; for example following a change of rein or on the oblique line from a half-volte just before returning to the track or even from counter-canter on the long side when going around the corner.

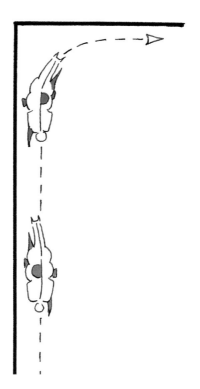

The flying change

Analysis of the official theory

Here is a summary of recommendations concerning training for flying changes:

Use of the seat
During the flying change the rider gives more driving aids and increases the weighting of the inside seat bone.
– Main teaching approaches
The rider asks for the flying change when changing the rein: on an oblique line from a half-volte, just before coming back to the track... flying change. On various diagonals when coming back to the track... flying change.
From counter-canter on the long side in the corner... flying change.

Problems and solutions
Horses that rush and escape after the flying change: since the cause is a sudden loss of balance, the rider must ask himself if the horse was correctly prepared and balanced and if the use of his aids was correct.

Horses that refuse to change, even when correctly prepared: make them do a flying change by jumping a pole placed on the ground across the diagonal, three metres before returning to the track.

Horses that start to have faults in the flying change: the most serious of these being to change in two beats with the hind legs changing late.

The cause is the rider's position. He must improve his seat and his aids. The solution mainly involves preparing the horse and riding it more strongly with the new outside rein and the new inside leg. The rider's new outside leg must also be used more strongly.

The flying change poses exactly the same problems of balance and locomotion as the canter strike-off for the simple reason that it is a canter strike-off from canter.

We have seen that the use of the seat to the inside encourages a canter strike-off by loss of balance to the inside shoulder. The result is that if the rider teaches the flying change, not only by sitting on the side of the new canter lead but also by turning in this direction, he throws the horse onto its new inside shoulder.

Under these conditions, it is hardly surprising that many horses only change in front or in two beats, or that others lose their balance and rush after the flying change or lastly that some literally refuse to change.

The analysis and the considered solutions are both uncertain and inconsequential:

The horse rushes after the flying change due to a sudden loss of balance. The rider must be better prepared, better balanced, and better at using his aids.

Excellent analysis if we draw the required conclusions: improved preparation, balance and the use of the aids, but this is rather unsurprisingly not the case! It is the whole approach to the movement that we must reconsider: from the role of our seat in general, and its use in asking for a canter strike-off and counter-canter in particular.

Horses that refuse to change canter lead even when correctly prepared.

If they refuse it is obvious that they have not been correctly prepared!

The solution, which involves having the horse go over a pole just before turning back to the track, has two disadvantages: it necessarily causes a flying change in two beats since after the jump the horse will firstly land on its forelegs. It is more of a trick and is therefore an admission of inability to provide a solution. What will happen once we take away the bar?

Horses that change in two beats: the cause is the rider. He must improve his seat and his aids. The solution involves using stronger aids.

Aids that achieve a poor result certainly must be improved. But not by increasing their strength. It would be better to change them!

The efficiency of the aids is more in terms of their type rather than their strength.

To sum up, this training approach to flying changes poses the following problems:

- It gives no specific preparation.
- It basically involves weighting to the inside and inversting the aids whilst turning in the direction of the new canter lead, which puts the horse in the worst conditions of balance to correctly change lead.
- In case of failure it recommends starting again with stronger aids - a source of tension, misunderstanding and worry.
- Since the place where the flying change takes place is easy to identify (when it comes back to the track or around a corner), the horse will become anxious and learn to anticipate or escape, which is never going to help give a good flying change. Often it will end up being impossible to calmly change rein. In the end this is not a method for teaching flying changes but a rushed way of "having a go" or even forcing things, with all the detrimental consequences that result.

Once again we will need gifted horses with a good temperament. And we can understand why so many horses are considered to be incapable of flying changes, whereas all of them can do it if we use a different approach.

An approach to the flying change

The flying change has a certain number of very specific problems. In order to effectively train it we have to identify and solve them as well as possible right from the start.

• Instant response

A flying change is asked for and executed in a fraction of a second. It therefore contains an element of surprise which, at least at the start, generates worry and tension. It is therefore a good idea to set up a progression that leads to the flying change just like we put a "cherry on the cake", calmly.

• Balance

Since a flying change is a canter strike-off from canter, if we are in canter to the right we must put the horse in a balance that is most favourable to cantering to the left. During the flying change the limbs on the right side have to support the whole horse and must come back to the ground twice in a row, starting with the right hind. We must therefore find a position and an exercise that weights the right lateral pair as far as possible.

• Locomotion

The most serious fault is a change in two beats, by anticipating the forelegs and so we must find a system that guarantees that the hind legs change first.

Canter to the right   Canter to the left

During the flying change from right to left, the limbs on the right side have to support the whole horse and must come back to the ground twice in a row – the rider can easily understand this by simulating a flying change himself.

Method

Preliminaries

The horse is already able to strike off easily from trot or walk on both reins on the inside or outside leg.

The horse is also confirmed in lateral work including renvers on the circle in walk, trot and canter.

On a large circle, start cantering on the inside leg:

1. Put the horse in a counter-bend then using a neck-rein with the outside rein, weight the inside seat and bring the horse's shoulders to the inside (the inside lateral pair are bearing the most weight).

Go back to walk in this situation. Immediately change the position of the legs with the inside leg pushing the haunches to the outside and the outside leg acting at the girth to ask the horse to canter on the outside leg in the renvers position on the circle.
Back to walk and reward.

2. Repeat this sequence on both reins until the horse totally understands it without hesitation or tension.

The horse therefore feels the balance that is useful for flying changes as well as the inversion of the aids, set up one after the other in a calm situation. It already does a virtual flying change.

Execution

Repeat the sequence. Use the same procedure but without going back to walk.

- Canter on the circle.
- Change the bend.
- Outside neck-rein.
- Weight the inside seat.
- Change the legs with a predominant action

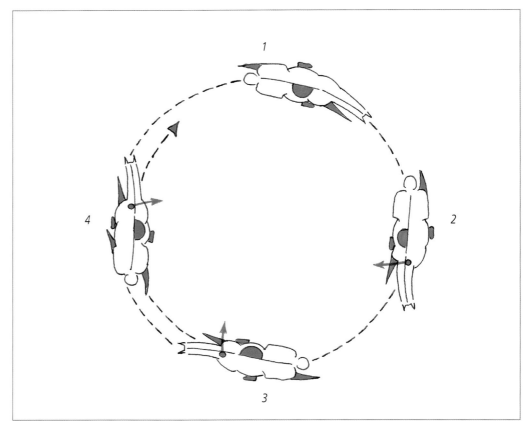

Teaching the flying change from right to left on the circle: from a right canter (1), the rider uses a counter-bend, acting with a left neck-rein (2) he weights his seat to the right (3) and changes the position of his legs to cause a strike-off to the outside leg in the renvers position (4).

of the inside leg. The horse knows what is coming next: renvers in canter- but this now implies that it changes leg and also that it does it behind first.

Sometimes the horse initially only changes its hind legs- go back to walk. Reward abundantly for this first step. Changing of the forelegs will come by itself later. If it does not come quickly enough, after a few disunited strides come back to walk and immediately go back into canter in the renvers position. Little by little this correction will no longer be necessary.

Summary

The horse has been well prepared to master this subject, and put in a position and balance that naturally imply a flying change led by the hind legs. There is no worrying surprise, the aids are changed one after the other- firstly the preparatory aids then the execution aids.

Indeed this method has other advantages: since the flying change occurs towards a lateral pair that bears as little weight as possible and that is going around the outside of a circle, the horse immediately learns to give it amplitude.

Working on the circle the rider can prolong the preparatory phase as long as he wants, repeating it again at any time and asking for the flying change wherever he wants on the circle. This avoids a geometric routine being set up that leads to the horse anticipating the flying change.

The first flying changes: the rider asks for the flying change to the outside on the circle, here from left to right. Initially cantering on the left the rider puts the horse in a counter-bend and weights his seat to the left...

Flying change from right to left: counter-bend to the left, seat to the right, the rider changes his legs .

... and by inversting the position of his legs he asks the horse to change into the renvers position to the right.

This procedure guarantees that the horse initially changes leg behind.

The horse once again touches the ground with the new outside hind leg...

... and continues to canter to the left in the renvers position. Photos: Laurioux

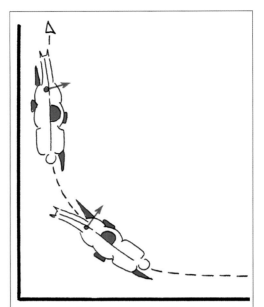

As soon as the horse masters the flying change to the outside on both reins on the circle, the rider can start the flying change on the straight line by asking for it to the outside just after going round the corner and gradually increasing the distance from the corner.

Progression

As soon as the horse masters the flying change to the outside on both reins on the circle, the rider can go on to the next step: starting the flying change on a straight line. Give priority to the inside leg in order to ensure straightness in the changes. Then ask for the flying changes closer together.

• After the corner: do not go too deep into the corner and reproduce the conditions set up on the circle asking for the flying change to the outside, just as you come out of the bend. Little by little the horse will learn to change leg further from the corner when staying straight along the wall.
• On a broken line off the track and back: these will be the first flying changes to the inside, but whilst maintaining the same preparatory approach. In counter-canter (bend to the inside) go around the corner and take the first part of the broken line coming in to the centre. To go back out to the track, turn using the inside neck-rein and weight the outside seat bone. Ask for a change to the inside just before starting the second line back to the track.

Do this first by coming off the track a long way and then gradually reduce the amount you come off the track until you can stay along the whole length of the long side.
• On the circle: repeat and bring the flying changes closer together without changing the bend. Perfect this on a figure of eight and a serpentine.
• On the straight line: repeat and bring the flying changes closer, paying particular attention to the straightness of the horse.

Overview

Reasoning that a horse turning to the right generally canters on the right leg and therefore concluding that we have to teach a canter strike-off to the right by weighting the right seat bone, and the flying change from left to right by turning to the right is typical of a rather hasty, simplistic and, in the end, detrimental deduction.

"Many mistakes are born of the abuse of truth." *(Voltaire)*

The requirements of locomotion and the laws of balance clearly tell us that the most logical and most dependable approach to teaching the flying change is to use a curve and to teach it to the outside rather than to the inside.

We simply have to observe horses at liberty or on the lunge to confirm this.

In counter-canter: when a horse does not stay on the outside leg, sometimes it correctly changes leg, but often it starts by disuniting in front when it is in a normal canter. Conversely, when it does not stay on the inside leg, either it changes correctly or it starts to disunite behind.

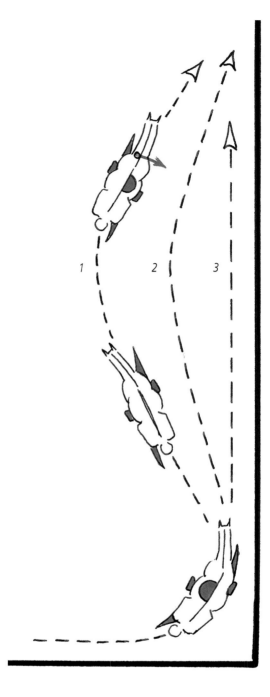

To teach the horse a flying change to the inside, the rider firstly asks for a flying change from a counter-canter on a broken line off the track and back out again (1). The balance conditions are the same as those of the flying change to the outside on a circle that the horse already knows. The rider will then reduce the size of the broken line off the track (2) until he can obtain the flying change whilst riding straight along the long side (3).

Cantering on a circle at liberty or on the lunge:
• when the horse changes leg to the inside it often initially does this by disuniting in front
• when it changes leg to the outside it often starts doing this by disuniting behind but never in front. Photo: Laurioux

Conclusion

After the counter-canter, this approach to the flying change once again confirms the suitability of weighting the seat to the outside in canter strike-offs.

This way of training flying changes is so effective that an instructor who masters it can use it to get his own students to train their own horses, under whatever circumstances

There is no need to get them to do hundreds of flying changes on drilled horses for them to become good at tricking gifted horses into doing them. They will learn whilst they educate their horse and it is a thrilling experience!

> The feature of a good training process is that it is applicable to all horses and fully transposable to training the rider.

Any equestrian principle that is not linked to the nature of the horse tends to have detrimental consequences, especially when it is held up as a dogma. This is the case of the overall bend of the horse, the so called "costal flexion" associated with a seat that is always weighted to the inside.

Making this illusion the key to training the horse, and believing that it can be maintained by weighting the inside seat bone, obliges the rider:

• to frequently sit on the opposite side to the movement requested from the horse (shoulder-in on a straight line, counter shoulder-in on the circle, haunches out on the circle, counter-canter)...
• to use his seat the wrong way in canter strike-offs and flying changes.

In the end, these incorrectly founded dogmas regularly put the rider out of phase with

the most elementary realities of balance and locomotion.

Such concepts are detrimental because they deprive us of natural solutions that are applicable to training all horses and because they are ipso facto limited to use on gifted subjects, although not without a considerable rate of failure. All of this does not sit well with the classical definition of dressage.

> If the rider wants to use aids that comply with the horse's nature, he should:
> • position the forehand and control the shoulders with the correct use of his hands...
> • activate the horse and channel the haunches using his legs and his seat, inducing variations in balance that are in line with the requirements of locomotion.
> • Avoid contradictory aid combinations.

TRANSITIONS
AND COLLECTION

Transitions

"Half-halts are used:

• *in transitions between paces*
• *to shorten the stride of a given pace..."*
"N.B.: The half-halt involves briefly closing the horse a little more between the aids of the seat, the leg and the hand then releasing the hand again."
"N.B.: The half-halt is not an isolated action it must be repeated as often as necessary until our goal is achieved."
(FN Guidelines for Riding and Driving, German Equestrian Federation, vol. 1, pp. 86-87.)

Analysis of the official theory

Remember that we are talking about training: educating a young horse to slow down in a pace and to change down a gait.

We can use the metaphor of a cyclist to shed light on the issue and eliminate any woolly ideas. Imagine that you are teaching a child to ride a bike and he is still quite a beginner. Imagine he starts on a long downhill road on which he quickly gains speed. Your child panics and cries: "I'm scared- what can I do?"

Points of comparison

• Anxiety and fear of new situations tends to scare horses just as much as young children.
• Riding a bike poses the same problems of balance as riding a horse. But they are easier to see because two wheels are less stable than four legs and the bike cannot compensate for the cyclist.
• When going downhill with the cyclist leaning on the handlebars, a bike mirrors the natural balance of a horse bearing more weight on the forehand and tending to gain speed.

• Like the horse's neck, the cyclist's torso is the only moving component that can be used for balance.
• As we proved with locomotion in the third chapter, during downward transitions the horse does not shorten its weight-bearing base and therefore does not engage its hindquarters. Consequently, like the cyclist's legs, those of the rider can only generate forwards movement. All of this means that the comparison is perfectly valid.

We can now apply the official dressage instructions to teaching the child on the bike.

Experiment with the official approach

• Your student is scared (tension) and holds on tightly to the handlebars (on the forehand). As a reassuring and skilful teacher you shout: "Don't worry, just do what I say!"
• "Keep leaning on the handlebars!" (Keeping the head low and of course fashionable overbending). "Put on the front brake!" (The famous "active hand": pressure that crushes the tongue, tensing the horse and causing or increasing overbending - therefore only acting by compressing the front end due to the low hand).
• "At the same time, push hard on the pedals!" (in order to ensure the sacrosanct and illusory engagement of the hind end.

Epilogue

In the following order, your student will probably end up going: on his nose, to the hospital and to another teacher, and maybe put off riding bikes forever! Your federal qualification as a teacher of classical bike riding will not be any help, even if you specialise with children in the gifted-breakneck category who have super-bikes.

From the point of view of balance, the horse and rider can be compared to a cyclist on a long downhill road: overloading the forehand tends to increase speed. Like the horse's neck, the rider's torso is the only moving component that can be used for balance. Just like the bike, the horse does not shorten its weight-bearing base during transitions and the cyclist's legs, like those of the rider, can only generate forwards movement.

Alternative

Basic slowing

- "Don't worry, listen to me!" Up to here, there is no difference. But this works even better if you have already proven trustworthy.
- "Stop peddling!" (In terms of locomotion and balance, pushing to slow down has no sense.)
- "Sit up and put your shoulders back as far as possible!" (Only lifting the neck will cause a change in balance that will help slowing.)
- "And now gradually put on the front brake!" (Repeated demi-arrêts increase the lifting of the neck until the horse slows as required, or even stops.)

Epilogue

This will have two consequences:

You will keep your students, even if they are moderately talented, and you will make them into respectable cyclists.

Which is the best method?

However, you will be brought to order by current orthodox thinking for prohibited lifting of the torso and the non-regulatory use of the legs!

One important consolation is that you can find some unambiguous support, including that of a certain Mr La Guérinière:

"The demi-arrêt is carried out by holding the curb hand close to you with the nails turned a little upwards without completely stopping the horse, but only holding and supporting the forehand when the horse leans on the bit or even when we want to increase ramener or collection."

"... if it leans too much on the hand, demi-arrêts must be more frequent and pronounced, only using the curb hand without any help of the calves or the legs; on the contrary we have to release the thighs because otherwise the horse will lean even more on the forehand."

A rider who does the official "half-halt" (in clear terms: pushes and pulls at the same time whilst weighing down on the horse's back) generally manages to stop the horse - this saves their face!

But the horse only obeys for three reasons:

- It knows by experience that it is the only way of stopping the rider pulling and crushing its tongue.
- It has four legs which makes it much more stable than the two wheels of a bike.
- Its instinct for preservation means that in spite of everything it will stay on its legs, even if it overloads the forehand to slow down and stop. The rider does not finish on his nose, but the horse does end up on its forehand.

However, transitions only have meaning and value for the rest of the horse's schooling if they help shift weight to the haunches. If this is not the case, we compromise the approach to collection from the outset.

Experimental illustration

In its issue dated May 2004, the *Cavallo* magazine published the results of an instructive experiment. Electronic sensors placed on the reins recorded the tension exerted on the horse's mouth during a transition from canter to halt.

A western trainer

The horse was ridden in a snaffle without a noseband. With high hands and without using his legs, the horse stops on the haunches with its poll open and remaining the highest point. The tension in the reins reaches 2.7kg per rein, applied only once.

Several dressage riders

Horses ridden in a snaffle with a double noseband as tight as possible. Using regulatory aids (seat and legs pushing onto low and active hands), the horses stop by dropping their poll, rather than the haunches. The riders use repeated half halts of up to 8 to 10 kg/rein and stop their horses with tensions of between 10 and 12.5 kg/rein.

This is the alternative: 5.4 kg on the corners of the mouth or (after 16 to 20 kg applied 4, 5 or 6 times) 25 kg on the tongue. In total, on the pretext of low hands and engagement of the hind quarters, official dressage shows us how to stop a horse by force and on its forehand.

During an experiment carried out by the "Cavallo" magazine, electronic sensors revealed that the western trainer Grischa Ludwig stops his horse from canter by acting upwards once on reins with a tension of 2.7 kg per rein. Photo: Cavallo

Dressage riders participating in the experiment repeatedly pulled on each rein with between 8 and 12.5 kg to stop their horses from canter. Photo: Cavallo

When the horse has been educated to engage its hindquarters and lower its haunches through the piaffe, the rider can use his legs to produce a collected halt. Transposing this to the cyclist metaphor, this corresponds to using a back-pedalling braking system.

The aim here is not to advocate western riding; it has its good points and its limitations. Having said that, we are totally entitled to ask one question: apart from bodybuilding its followers and sacrificing them to its rites, what is the purpose of competitive dressage?

In his last book, Nuno Oliveira wrote:

"Current dressage riders would be well advised to wonder how their horse would behave on a mountain path, crossing natural ditches or fences, or if they went back in time and had to defend their life with the reins in one hand and a sword or sabre in the other."

Lifting of the neck, asked for only by the hand (distinctly to start with and increasingly discreetly afterwards) is therefore not the heresy denounced by the fans of low hands, but an absolute necessity for balance - at least for all downward transitions.

> The choice is ours: either the rider uses the poll as a handbrake (without a thought for balance) or he uses the neck as a balancing pole.

The advanced halt

Your cyclist has gained in experience, he has grown in motivation and knowledge. You can now teach him to stop as he wants and virtually without using the brake.

Firstly you have to make some significant modifications to the bike: installing a back-pedalling braking system (our grandfathers' bikes often had this). On a nice fast downhill stretch you will tell your student: "Sit up and shift your weight to the pedals. Now pedal backwards!" He will easily and quickly stop by braking the rear wheel and without using the brakes on the handlebars.

We can transpose this: the use of the legs in downward transitions is only justified for collected halts (on the haunches) - what past masters called a parade or even a falcade. Confirmation of this from La Guérinière:

"The halt is the effect produced by the action we have by holding the horse's head and the other parts of the forehand with the curb hand and at the same time gently bringing the haunches under the horse with our calves so that the whole body of the horse is supported in balance and on its haunches."

"... by gently using your calves, you must place your shoulders back a little and hold the curb rein a little firmer until the halt is achieved."

But this is only possible to consider on three conditions:

• The horse has been previously educated to engaging the hindquarters and lowering its haunches through the piaffe (installing the back-pedalling system).
• The halt requires the neck to be raised to the right level: shifting the weight to the haunches (straightening the torso and pressing on the pedals).
• The rider has a clearly different use of the legs from that for forwards movement. Legs at the girth to put the horse forward (pedalling), legs back to stop, rein-back and collect (back-pedalling).

Fashionable objections

Judgement of this is peremptory and comes across as an absolute truth: "Raising the head hollows the back!" This is a simplistic assertion which does not reflect anatomy - a bad habit. Two cases must be distinguished:

1. The horse that raises its head and hollows

In general this happens with thin and weak necks. Hollowing of the neck occurs as follows:

- Shortening of the muscles to raise the head and the poll extensors (complexus).
- This leads to the dropping of the withers. The rib cage drops between the shoulders. The lifting muscles of the base of the neck lengthen (angular muscles of the shoulder).
- Consequently, the whole dorso-lumbar line tends to hollow. The illio-spinal muscles are contracted, the back becomes concave, the haunches become horizontal and the hindquarters move out behind (the horse stands out behind).

There is no doubt that horses of this type hollow their back. But it is not the rider causes this by raising the head, because it is the horse that takes the initiative: it goes above the hand, evades the contact and rushes.

These horses will be worked with an extension of the neck so as to regain their natural roundness and return the back to the right position. All of the basic work will be carried out like this (lateral work, transitions and rein back): an unavoidable but temporary compromise until we have sufficient remodelling of the neck (developing of the muscles in its base). From this point on, the rider will be able to ask for gradual lifting of the neck, repeating an extension every time the horse hollows and goes above the hand.

2. The horse that raises its head and lifts the base of its neck

In general: strong and short necks. These are horses that lean on the hand and that throw themselves on the forehand.

Using demi-arrêts (repeated lifting of the hands followed by a "descente de main") the rider stops the horse leaning on the hand and asks it to raise its head and neck.

It is the angular muscles of the shoulder which contract and raise the base of the neck. The lifting muscles of the head and the extensor muscles of the poll (complexus) are virtually not involved. From the top of the shoulders to the base of the spine, by shortening, the angular muscles of the shoulder raise the withers and the ribcage: the horse grows. (See horses at liberty, when they are showing off: they raise their whole forehand with their neck virtually vertical and the poll open.)

The front insertions of the illio-spinal muscles move back. These muscle groups release and give the back and haunches the freedom it needs to flex by shortening the abdominal muscles therefore facilitating engagement of the hind legs under the horse's body (for the collected halt, the piaffe, very collected canter and the pirouette).

Overview

> We can say that the muscles used to lift the base of the neck and the abdominal muscles work in synergy.

Locomotion is there to show this:

- In a free canter (on the right leg), at every stride the neck stretches from the weight-bearing phase of the left hind leg through to the weight-bearing phase of the right foreleg (propulsion phase). It then rises throughout the weight-bearing phase of the right foreleg through to the weight-bearing phase of the left hind leg: in other words before and during all of the flight phase and the engagement of the hind legs.

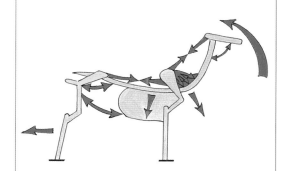

Negative consequences of hollowing the neck

A horse that raises its neck and hollows, does so with its whole top-line. The withers drop, the back becomes concave and the hind legs move out behind.
This horse will be worked by extending its neck until there is sufficient development of the muscles at the base of its neck.

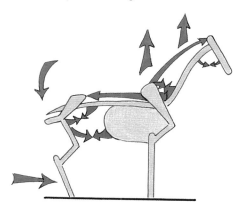

Positive consequences of lifting the neck

The horse that lifts its head and the base of its neck, lifts its withers and its rib cage. The illio-spinal muscles release and give the back and haunches the freedom to flex therefore facilitating engagement of the hind legs under the horse's body.

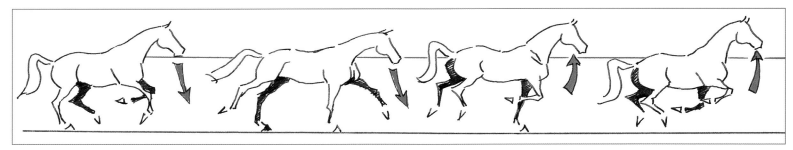

In every aspect of the horse's locomotion, the muscles that lift the base of the neck and the abdominal muscles work in synergy: the hindquarters engage as the neck is raised; they lengthen as it is lowered.

It is the lifting of the neck that allows the horse to bring its hind legs a long way forward under its body, especially when jumping on the take-off stride and when landing on the ground.

• When jumping. The horse lifts its neck for the take-off stride. This movement allows it to engage its hind legs, collect its strength and raise its shoulders to the angle of the jump trajectory. To bascule over the jump, the horse lifts its neck even more. This movement allows it to bring its hind legs under it and back onto the ground after the front legs have landed.
• A stallion that piaffes excitedly at its stable door lowers its haunches and engages its hind legs, lifting its neck as far as possible. It never lowers it and it never overbends.

> Lifting of the base of the neck is not only a necessity for balance - it is also a condition for useful engagement of the hind legs.

La Guérinière clearly expresses his views concerning the *demi-arrêt*.

"... and since through this aid we flex the poll and we support the forehand, at the same time we CONSEQUENTLY oblige the horse to lower its haunches."

The dressage manual (B1, page 139) states the contrary:

> *"Lifting of the neck results from the increased flexion of the hind legs."*

It takes its inspiration from G. Steinbrecht:

> *"... if the action of the rider's legs is correct, the horse will do this itself. Firstly looking to escape or relieve the effort when pushed from behind, it is held in front and therefore compressed on itself."*

Which at least has the merit of being clear: lifting the neck is considered as an evasion from the outset. Collection is considered in terms of compression obtained by force. The most extraordinary aspect remains the fact that all of these peremptory statements and muscled concepts are given with the alibi of being in compliance with the principles of La Guérinière!

It is easy to claim that horses grow themselves when they need to collect, as asserted by official dressage. But how can we believe this when we also see that it is only reserved for horses with good conformation, born with their necks coming high out of the withers and is careful not to show us what happens with the others. Even when riding these horses whose conformation already puts them in a very favourable position for collection, very often it manages to ruin their natural balance by compression and overbending to finally produce a shuffle on the forehand instead of a piaffe.

Official dressage is therefore unable to prove its theories.

> Anatomy, locomotion, balance and common sense confirm the decisive role of the hand in raising the neck during transition work and when approaching collection, in line with La Guérinière's teachings.

Rein-Back

A summary of official recommendations for asking a horse to rein-back.
Use of the aids.

> • *"The rider uses his weight (on both seat bones) and his legs to put the horse forwards."*
> *"The rider's legs are placed in position to control and stop the horse's haunches from escaping."*
> • *"When the horse responds and is going to move forward, the rider 'feels' both reins and gives the active hand aids. At this more advanced stage a hand which does not release will be sufficient. In both cases the energy created forwards is converted into backwards movement."*
> • *"As soon as the horse responds by moving backwards the rider's hands lighten, although they must maintain contact with the horse's mouth." (B1, page 98)*

Analysis of the official theory

The seat and the legs ask for forwards movement? And yet we want the horse to go backwards! All horses fear reining back and only do it themselves if they have no alternative.

Indeed a horse cannot see where it is going when it moves backwards. For this fearful animal with a highly developed flight instinct, this means: going to something unknown where there might be all sorts of danger. It is certainly not a time to use contradictory aids.

As for the position of the legs, intended to prevent the haunches escaping, remember that we have seen that the horse must be straightened using the front end.

It is therefore your hand that must bring the shoulders in front of the haunches using a lateral effect and reversing the neck bend if necessary (neck-rein). Trying to hold a horse straight or straighten a horse using the legs is simply addressing the effects instead of dealing with the cause (bending of the whole spine and weighting of the outside shoulder).

This image of rein-back, involving bouncing the forwards movement off an "active hand" is appealing for an engineering mind but comes up against two problems.

It does not in any way correspond to the reality for the horse. Rein-back is not a forwards movement transformed into a backwards movement. In terms of locomotion these are therefore two diametrically opposed mechanisms. The horse pushes itself forwards by extending the weight-bearing hind leg, moving it behind the vertical plumb-line (contracting the illio-spinal muscles, the buttock muscles, the ischio-tibial muscles and the gastrocnemial muscles). It moves backwards by flexing its weight-bearing hind leg, moving it in front of its vertical plumb-line (contracting the psoa, crural and abdominal muscles).

Lastly, the horse is not a car: the horse that you are training to rein back does not have a reverse gear. And if a car does not have reverse gear, you can always try accelerating in first gear and putting on the handbrake at the same time! You may break everything, but there is no way you will go backwards!

Reining-back by compression

Dressage manuals ask for the rein-back by compressing the horse between the driving aids and the holding aids.

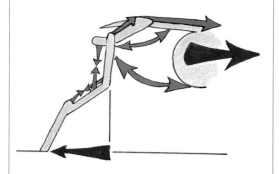

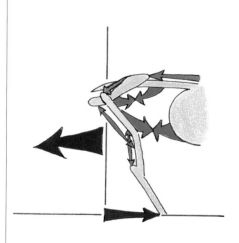

In terms of locomotion, forwards movement and the rein-back are two diametrically opposed mechanisms involving different muscle groups: the horse propels itself forward by extending the weight-bearing hind leg, moving it behind the vertical plum-line (diagram above). It moves backwards by flexing the weight-bearing hind leg, moving it in front of the vertical plumb-line (diagram below).

In clear terms the official method involves pulling and pushing at the same time.

Two cases can occur:

• A generous horse that respects the legs will try to move forward and, since it does not understand the backwards effect of the hand, it will run through it. In the end we will punish it for having obeyed the legs, and we all know the detrimental consequences of that!
• A placid horse that is not very sure about the impulsive role of the legs will be quick to listen to the hands, and all too happy to neglect the legs and go behind them. Not really a cause for rejoicing!

In addition, according to official instructions, as soon as the horse starts to rein-back the rider must reduce the strength of the reins. This is good, but means that the horse will continue to move backwards with a predominant action of the legs. Does this mean that more active legs should cause an acceleration of the rein-back? If you want to teach a horse to no longer move forward this would be a good technique!

Under these conditions:

• Asking for rein-back through compression satisfies current equestrian prejudice but in no way corresponds to the horse's needs (psychology, locomotion, balance).
• Why should the horse rein-back using seat and leg aids that are fundamentally reserved for forwards movement? The horse that reins back in this way learns to doubt the impulsive role of the legs and will remember this when it comes to collection and particularly the piaffe.
• How can we be surprised that so many horses rein-back so badly or obstinately refuse to rein-back?

We can understand recommendations for caution such as: "*Don't rein-back too early...*

and limit yourself to a few steps". With this concept, training a horse to rein-back generates many problems and contributes so little, that it will be truly wise to say: "*If you do it this way, you might as well not do it at all*".

Alternative

In terms of balance and locomotion, forwards movement and the rein-back are diametrically opposed. Common sense therefore means that the aids that ask for them must be strictly the opposite.

• Forwards: "legs, without hands..."
• Rein-back: "hands, without legs..."

According to their conformation, not all horses can approach the rein-back in the same way.

Elementary rein-back for horses that hollow their neck

With these horses that tend to go above the hand and hollow their neck and back, and even move their hind legs out behind, rein-back is particularly good but impossible to achieve without the right approach. Riders will not consider reining back until they have correctly trained the horse to lengthen its neck only in response to the hand.

Assistance from the ground
The rider will ask the horse to lengthen its neck, relieving the weight on the horse's back by moving his shoulders forward and placing his legs back (passive: simple code). Simultaneously, an assistant on the ground will give little taps with the whip on the front legs and then on the horse's chest. As soon as the horse makes a move backwards, reward it. This process is explicitly described by La Guérinière.

Reining back with extension of the neck

According to their conformation, not all horses can start the rein-back in the same way: with horses that go above the hand and hollow their neck and back, the rider will ask for the rein-back with an extension of the neck until he remodels the whole top-line (diagram above). With horses suitable for raising the base of the neck, the rein-back will be carried out by lifting the neck, causing an initial shifting of the weight back over the haunches (diagram below).

Rein-back by lifting the neck

Collected rein-back

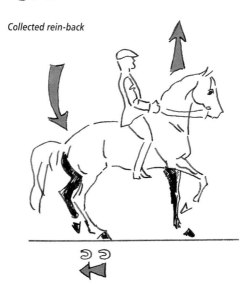

For the collected rein-back, the rider filters the backwards movement by repeated touches of both legs, so that the strides shorten. The horse then reins back in a sort of small piaffe with increased flexion of all of its joints and a shortening of its weight-bearing base.

As things advance the rider will no longer need assistance from the ground. The horse will rein-back by lengthening its neck and rounding its back, simply when the rider changes his position with a contact on the reins and without the legs being active at all.

For these horses, the elementary rein-back cannot be considered as a movement that puts it on its haunches, but as an overall corrective gymnastic exercise. It would be absurd to limit this to a few steps. As long as the horse rein-backs slowly, relaxed, round and straight, it will gradually give 10, 15, 20 metres of rein-back without any problem.

When this work has helped to improve the whole top-line, and when the horse stays in the hand, it will be able to start reining-back in an increasingly raised attitude.

Elementary rein-backs for horses that tend to raise the base of the neck

Prolonging the aids used to slow down, beyond the halt: the rider grows, brings his shoulders back and places his legs backwards (simple code) by supporting the hand he increases the lifting of the neck until the horse starts to rein back. Move forwards again and reward.

As the horse gains in experience it will gradually rein-back on the slightest action of the hand. Growing itself, it will allow the rider to flex its poll as long as it does not drop.

For these horses, the large majority, the rein-back is an outstanding way of moving the weight back to the haunches - as long as we use natural aids which lift the withers rather than contradictory aids which overbend and drop the horse on the shoulders.

The collected rein-back

A correct elementary rein-back moves the horse's weight back over its haunches by raising the neck with the corollary of tending to flex all of the joints in the hindquarters. In order to have a really effective rein-back and to use it in the approach to a piaffe, we have to collect it.

Ask for a rein-back using the usual aids: shoulders back, lifting the hands with passive legs that are positioned back. As soon as the rein-back starts, give repeated touches with both legs so that they filter the backwards movement and shorten the strides. The rein-back can also be collected by asking for it on curved lines. Combine the aids for rein-back, an inside neck-rein and an isolated leg guiding the haunches on the curve. This gymnastic exercise increases the weight to the inside haunch and increases the flexion of the corresponding hind leg. Past masters called this: the *"foule en arrière"*.

The collected rein-back is very effective: increased flexion of all the joints and shortening of the weight-bearing base. This often produces a high-energy diagonalisation of the rein-back, a sort of small piaffe, whilst reining back with very short strides. But this is obviously only possible on three conditions:

• The horse must be very light to the legs.
• For this rein-back, the legs act in a place that is different for that used for forwards movement.
• The elementary rein-back must have naturally been taught without legs. Popular French wisdom says:

"If you waste all your cartridges shooting at sparrows, you won't have any left when you need to shoot at a wolf."

Overview

Rein-back is much more than a movement to be used in homeopathic doses simply because only three to six strides are asked for in dressage tests.

When well understood, the rein-back is a fantastic overall gymnastic exercise to be systematically carried out using a range of transitions to control the horse's balance. But for this to be true, it must be taught:

• With a hand that supports and rebalances instead of pulling (a fatality with low hands).
• And without legs (to be consistent and to not undermine impulsion).

Quite a few of the great past masters taught the rein-back without any use of the legs:

"… with a snaffle rein in each hand, he lifts the arms again acting on the corners of the mouth upwards so as to cause the rein-back by shifting the weight back to the hindquarters." *(Faverot de Kerbrech)*

"The rider therefore focuses on initially putting the head straight and engages the horse in a rein-back by equal and increasing tension on the reins. The head, when yielding, puts pressure on the neck which runs through the shoulders and is communicated to the whole body. Through the gradual increase of this pressure, the forehand lightens and we shift part of the weight back to the hindquarters which itself has to move back in order to relieve itself of this effort."
(Ludwig Hünersdorf)

"… in order to accustom the horse to reining-back with ease, after having halted we have to hold the curb rein, with the nails upwards as if we want to halt again, and when it obeys, in other words it steps back one or two steps, we must release our hand…"
(La Guérinière)

La Guérinière, close to the last teachings of Baucher and contrary to the theories of modern dressage. This is definitely a recurring theme!

The Piaffe

After a good description of the piaffe, the reader's attention is drawn to the following points.

Definition *(B2, page 64)*
"Most of the horse's weight is shifted to the hindquarters which are flexed, whilst the forelegs are lightened."

"The back muscles work and the forehand grows distinctly, the poll remains the highest point."

PREPARATION IN-HAND

Equipment *(B2, page 73)*
"Snaffle, cavesson, saddle and/or surcingle, side reins, leg boots (front and back) a guiding rein or a lunge line."

"The trainer needs a special whip for working in hand, at least 1.5 metres long, flexible and quite firm. He needs protective shoes (without spurs) and gloves."

Approach *(B2, page 75)*
"Whatever method is used, the guiding rein must stop the horse from moving forwards through sufficient actions upwards and backwards.
Associated with propulsive aids, these holding aids cause collection and the flexing of the haunches."

Problems *(B2, pages 76 and 77)*
"If the horse leans on the bit and avoids collecting by falling on the shoulders, it is necessary for a short period of time to use a training aid. But its use must be accompanied by strengthened propulsive aids."

"If the horse jumps to the side or escapes with its haunches, it will lose the rhythm. This is mainly caused by the incorrect position of the trainer. He must stand as far forwards as possible at the horse's head."

Horse that escapes
"… put an assistant in front of it who holds the lunge and the cavesson. As a last resort, with a horse that is forwards to this extent, frequently ask for a few steps of rein-back."

Ridden work *(FN Guidelines for Riding and Driving, German Equestrian Federation, vol. 2, page 65.)*
"From halt, the horse is ridden forwards in a 'piaffe-walk'. With both legs the rider activates the horse's hindquarters and approaches them nearer to the centre of gravity. With half-halts taking and releasing with a repeated action of the hand on a gentle contact, the rider transfers the weight from the forehand to the haunches."

"This collection in a 'piaffe-walk' must firstly be carried out along the length of the wall to stop the haunches from escaping, and an assistant must provide support with a long and quite stiff whip."

"A perfectly schooled horse will be able to produce 15 steps of piaffe in rhythm and balance and advancing by at most two hoof-prints."

Analysis of the official theory

Definition of piaffe

As shown in the first chapter: a correct piaffe requires verticality of the weight-bearing foreleg and distinct and active engagement of the hindquarters. The horse is at least in a "horizontal balance" that is unstable: equal distribution of weight on the limbs. This quality of piaffe is rarely seen, so it is rather exaggerated to claim that the haunches bear the largest share of the load. A very good piaffe requires even greater engagement, which this time really puts the horse more on the haunches than on the shoulders. It then takes maximum elevation of the shoulders and is as expressive as is possible to achieve.

The back muscles work, in any case, in all exercises and all paces - good or bad, this way or that way, but they work!

In a good piaffe, the dorsal muscles are extended due to the dorso-lumbar rounding and flexion of the haunches. Consequently the muscles which supply most of the work are the psoa, crural and abdominal muscles ,rather than the dorsal muscles.

Short and thick dorsal muscles are therefore from this point of view a handicap. "Muscling the back" is an obsession without any basis. What we must aim for is the rounding of the back, and it is indeed the abdominal muscles which can achieve this rather than the dorsal ones.

The forehand must grow and the poll must remain the highest point: this is indisputable. But this will of course require that the horses do not work constantly overbent and that judges penalise this terrible fault in each figure, including the piaffe. Which is currently not the case.

Equipment

The arsenal recommended by the manuals seem to imply rather heavy handed explana-

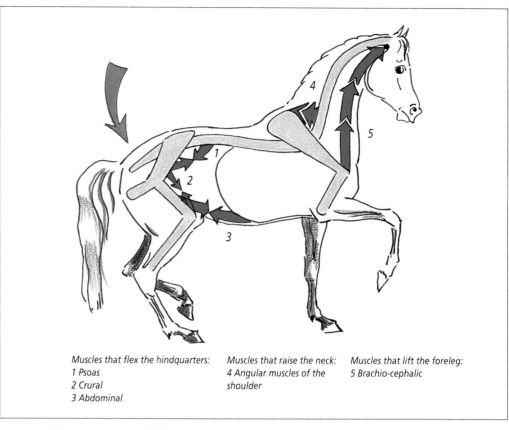

Muscles that flex the hindquarters:
1 Psoas
2 Crural
3 Abdominal

Muscles that raise the neck:
4 Angular muscles of the shoulder

Muscles that lift the foreleg:
5 Brachio-cephalic

In a good piaffe, the psoa, crural and abdominal muscles round the dorso-lumbar segment and cause the flexing of the haunches. The base of the neck lifts, the brachio-cephalic muscles pull the shoulders upwards.

tions backed up by leg protections, means of restraint and stiff whips, which does not conjure up the idea of a friendly learning approach. Especially at this stage in the horse's training, the rider should be able to place his horse's head without side reins and activate it without a specially designed whip. To be frank, this admission is certainly very significant and worrying.

Planned approach

The simultaneous use of "propulsive aids" and "holding aids" already used to put the horse on the bit, for the costal flexion, the half-halt, transitions, the halt and the rein-back are now meant to put the horse into piaffe.

This authoritative and compressive approach cannot be justified in terms of either psychology, balance or locomotion. On one hand, the use of authoritarian instruments is a sign that the result is neither natural nor guaranteed. On the other hand, seeing the piaffes that are generally produced in dressage competitions, we simply have to believe that we can do better than that.

Problems encountered

For a horse that leans on the hand and falls on the forehand the manual recommends more training aids and pushing harder.

This simply adds further restrictive equipment, whose success is certainly not guaranteed, to the problems created by the initial restraint.

A horse that escapes through the haunches does so because it is crooked and worried. Changing the trainer's position can prove useful but above all it is that of the horse that we have to correct. For example a horse whose haunches escape to the right when approaching the piaffe, is imposing its natural flexion to the right. We have to straighten its neck and piaffe it in a shoulder-in to the right on the right rein and on the left rein we must piaffe with the shoulders close to the wall and with a bend to the left.

Anything else is simply a trick which tries to cancel the effects but which in no way deals with the causes.

A horse that escapes is doing this either because it is on the shoulders or because it is scared of the whip, or even both at the same time. Putting someone in front of it to hold it adds to the restraint and does not solve any of the basic problems. One person on the guiding rein, one behind with a whip and another in front - how can we be satisfied with needing so much equipment and a whole team to educate a horse in piaffe?

This is more about determination than science.

Ridden work

The famous "piaffe-walk" asked by legs that push (often spurs) assisted by a stiff whip and hands which give and take (in fact pulling) overbends the horse more often than it collects it. In addition it often deteriorates the collected walk.

If a horse is perfectly schooled, why stop at 15 steps? Because the grand prix requires 12? This makes no sense.

Before being a movement imposed in certain tests, the piaffe must be a beneficial exercise for the whole of the horse's schooling.

Such an essential gymnastic exercise cannot be limited to 15 steps - unless we admit that it is laboriously and incorrectly approached. The simple fact of having to permanently push hard and constrain the horse firmly prove that we are missing the conditions for a correct piaffe.

> When correctly understood, the piaffe is an outstanding demonstration of relaxation, impulsion and balance. Which has the corollary of being carried out in légèreté: descente de main and descente de jambes (see glossary).
> Under these conditions the number of steps is not a problem. 15, 30, 50? Compression and inappropriate balance are what set the limits both in quality and quantity.

Alternative

So what conditions do we need to be able to piaffe?

Relaxation

When a horse piaffes itself it is often when it is very excited. By nature, this air therefore contains the beginnings of the risk of disorder, panic and even evasions. It is therefore essential to approach it with a constant concern for relaxation.

However, nothing worries the horse (a symbol of freedom) more than feeling it is in a trap between a whip that it would like to flee from and side reins, a cavesson and hands that prevent it from doing so. The use of restraining devices and compression between the "propulsive aids" and "holding aids" should therefore be excluded from the outset.

Impulsion

To get his horse to piaffe a rider needs an enormous amount of impulsion: an explosive desire to immediately go forward on the slightest touch of the legs at the girth (lightness to the legs).

Locomotion

Since the piaffe is a vibrant and high energy diagonalisation, what could be more natural than increasing impulsion as far as possible through repeated transitions from halt to trot? Giving the lesson of the leg again if necessary. Mixing this with a return to calm.

Balance

To get his horse to piaffe a rider needs to lighten the shoulders as far as possible and to shift the weight back to the haunches (lightness to the hand). Since the piaffe is a diagonalisation on the haunches, what could be more logical than to use repeated collected rein-backs (diagonal pace that shifts the horse's weight backwards onto its haunches).

But to do this we must have obtained an elementary rein-back by lifting the neck and without any use of the legs. So no side reins which prohibit any change in attitude, but hands which help the front end to grow.

Straightness

We can recall that G. Steinbrecht called the shoulder-in : "positioning in trot". Aligning one diagonal with the axis of movement, it encourages engagement of the hind leg which is basically involved in propelling the horse and induces the lowering and weighting of the inside haunch. It therefore encourages diagonalisation of the movement and collection.

Since it also cancels out any tendency for the haunches to escape, it straightens the horse and is a partial gymnastic exercise, which tends to collect the horse one side after another.

Transitions between walk, trot and halt in a shoulder-in position will therefore be particularly effective in approaching the piaffe.

It is therefore frequent transitions in shoulder-in, then between trot (diagonal impulsion) and rein-back (diagonalised balance) that are most logical and most effective to teach a horse to piaffe.

However, training a piaffe by compression from a shortened walk cannot be justified at all. This only gets relatively poor results and then only with particularly gifted horses.

An approach to the piaffe -sequence

1. Trot – halt – trot transitions

Repeat these transitions making sure that the horse moves off "at the slightest touch of the leg" (repeat the lesson of the leg every time necessary) and stops whilst remaining light to the hand (growing the front end by demi-arrêts).

Carrying out these transitions in shoulder-in will ensure straightness and will encourage engagement of the inside hind.

2. Trot – rein-back - trot transitions

Work on these transitions in the same spirit as the previous ones. Look for an instant change, without any hesitation, between an energetic trot and a collected rein-back. Do this until the horse happily moves between these two diagonal paces without hesitation, tension or loss of straightness.

3. Initial diagonalisation

The more fluid and the more generous the transitions between trot – rein-back – trot, the closer the rider will be able to bring them together. It will soon be possible to do so every few strides.

Initial diagonalisation: instead of compressing the horse on the spot, the rider teaches it to piaffe by repeating transitions.
Photo: Laurioux

Priority to balance. Flexion of the poll will come later. Photo: Slawik

The more the horse understands, the more the preparatory phase is shortened and the more the rider can prolong the time he piaffes and look to increase its expression. Photo: Laurioux

When the horse repeats a certain number of transitions of this type over a few metres' distance it is ready to move on to the next stage:

• Whenever it reins-back the horse knows that it will very soon have to move forward in trot.
• There will come a point in time when this calm obsession of moving forward into trot will lead it to anticipate: the horse will tend to piaffe in its rein-back (reminder of the collected rein-back).
• The rider will encourage this activity, maintaining it by touching with the leg that remains backwards (the position for collection) but filtering the forward movement (very shortened strides) and sitting deep in the saddle (shoulders back) making sure that the neck remains raised (demi-arrêts).

• Be content with a few strides then move forward and reward.

The real problem is not to know how to ask for piaffe, but how to prepare it since a horse that is ready will offer the piaffe by itself: let it do this and encourage it.

With horses that escape through the haunches, systematically piaffing in shoulder-in straightens and strengthens the engagement of the inside hind. With horses that are hesitant or lazy: stop the piaffe as soon as it loses its energy by moving forward energetically in trot, using the whip, instead of using more leg. Then immediately go back to piaffe. Move forwards and reward.

The lesson of the leg remains applicable: the whip must be used only as a reminder of moving forwards rather than used for piaffe.

With horses that lose balance or tend to escape: rein-back often before the piaffe (collected rein-back). With excitable horses: piaffe often and very little, walk forwards or even halt, full rest after each sequence.

4. Perfecting

• The more the horse understands the more it will answer the specific aids for piaffe and the more the preparation phase will be shortened.
• Increase and prolong the descente de main and descente de jambes so that the horse piaffes whilst free but "under surveillance", on "conditional freedom".
• Once the correction has been established, the rider will look to prolong the time for which he piaffes and ask for more expression.

Only at this stage can small touches of the spur be useful to ask for more activity in response to the legs.

• As long as the horse retains its desire to move forward, the piaffe can be shortened until it takes place rigorously on the spot or even moving backwards.

• The piaffe will firstly be worked on along the wall, on both reins, then on the inside track and at any point on the arena.

Overview

In line with its other concepts, official dressage searches for collection by compression from halt and walk. Under these conditions the approach to piaffe needs a lot of equipment and only very rarely achieves a correct result, even with outstanding horses - the others are not even considered!

"Only horses suitable for this work must be chosen for high school dressage. Horses with conformation faults or with difficult temperaments require a very long and laborious period of schooling, often with unsatisfactory results!"
(B2, page 25)

And yet virtually all horses can give a respectable piaffe if we use more natural and therefore more correct methods.

The modelling clay metaphor

To transform a hardened block of modelling clay (an unschooled horse) into an easy-to-mould mass of clay that can be moved in all directions (a schooled horse) a rider must form a shape that has an unstable balance (collection). To do this you start by bending and kneading the block until it becomes malleable (relaxation and flexibility). Then you gradually roll it in every direction... from left to right (curves and lateral work)... from front to back (transitions and rein-back)... until you get a virtually perfect sphere, with immediate and total mobility (piaffe).

There is a reciprocal relationship: if unstable balance (piaffe) gives total mobility, it is by developing this mobility (transitions) that we arrive at an unstable balance.

However well equipped and clever you are, by successive compression between two boards you will spend a lot of energy without ever achieving a comparable result.

An approach to piaffe by static compression from halt or walk is like trying to produce the effect by force, without knowledge of the natural causes or how to set them up rationally.

Horses that collect improve in mobility and it is by developing its mobility that the rider collects a horse.

The piaffe, a diagonal air, must result from complete mobility between:

• The trot (diagonal movement + activity): "lightness to the legs"

• and the rein-back (diagonal movement + balance on the haunches): "lightness to the hand"

This method generally does not involve in-hand work since the rider has many more possibilities in terms of transitions when he is in the saddle than when he is on foot. If we do use in-hand work it will be on the same basis: transitions in shoulder-in and frequent transitions between trot and rein-back.

No légèreté, no piaffe.

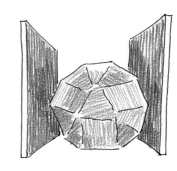

The schooled horse resembles a blob of modelling clay which you have shaped into a ball and which therefore can easily be moved in any direction. The only way to achieve this is by bending and kneading the blob and rolling it in all directions (developing the horse's complete mobility). If you squeeze the blob again and again between two boards (work the horse by compressing it between driving and restraining aids) you will never get a ball.

The Passage

Analysis of the official theory

"Like the piaffe, the horse raises its forelegs to the horizontal and the haunches flex and rhythmically propel the horse's body forwards."

"To produce a beautiful passage all of the horse's back muscles contract and the lumbar back is flexed like in piaffe."

"Naturally since this is the highest degree of collection, it must give the impression of total freedom." (B2, page 68)

Approach

"The passage can be developed from a collected trot, from the piaffe-walk, from the piaffe and from the walk. It is up to the rider to study his horse and choose the best suited method." (B2, page 69)
"Initially in passage, as for piaffe, assistance from the ground can be very useful." (FN Guidelines for Riding and Driving, German Equestrian Federation, vol. 2, page 70.)

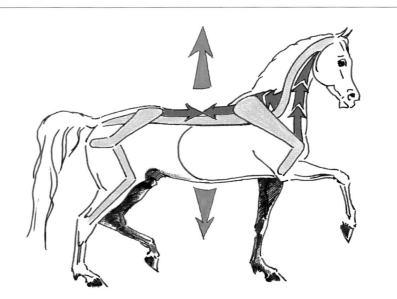

In passage, the horse raises the base of the neck with the brachio-cephalic muscles pulling the shoulders upwards. As opposed to what must happen in piaffe, the haunches do not flex since the hind legs do not come further under the horse's body. The back muscles shorten and the back does not arch. Simplifying things we could say that the horse passages with its dorsal muscles and piaffes with its abdominal muscles.

Definition of passage

Since photographs have been around for over 150 years, there are plenty of documents on this.

Those taken of passage constantly show that the horse never shortens its natural diagonal weight-bearing base, and that it even often opens it from behind (weight-bearing front leg vertical, weight-bearing hind leg behind the tip of the haunches).

Indeed this often corresponds to very expressive passages.

Consequence:

• Propelling the body forwards, the haunches do not flex since the hind legs do not come further under the body.
• The back muscles do not contract more than the abdominals, especially since the back does not arch - as opposed to what must happen in piaffe.
• The passage is not the highest degree of collection, by a long way, since the horse does not shorten its diagonal weight-bearing base. This is why we see more respectable passages than correct piaffes.
• Simplifying things we could say that the horse piaffes with its abdominal muscles and passages with its dorsal muscles.

Overall, all of this accumulates a lot of inconsistencies and fallacies in terms of locomotion since, apart from their diagonal mechanism, passage and piaffe have nothing in common. This is the very reason why transitions between these two airs are a major difficulty.
In fact, there are two types of collection:

1. The first basically results from a growing of the neck and increased lifting of the shoulders movement. This is why Spanish walk is so good at preparing for this.

This collection is achieved in forwards movement and without any shortening of the weight-bearing base. The passage is the best example.

2. The second adds the active engagement of the hindquarters under the horse's body to the raising of the front end with flexion of the back and lowering of the haunches. This type of collection can only be achieved with greatly shortened strides or on the spot. Piaffe is the best example as well as the canter required for a pirouette.

Ways of teaching passage

Since it is a stylised trot, passage can be obtained from trot, provided the latter is naturally expressive. Passage can also be obtained from piaffe since the horse already has the diagonal movement, in a greater degree of collection.

However, since it has no direct link with either the trot or the piaffe, we can question whether it is ideal to teach passage from either.

As for support from someone on the ground: the horse will only increase its activity (often by becoming tense) because it is scared of the whip and it will reduce its activity as soon as it is out of the whip's range.

This is one of the reasons why many horses give a good impression when they are close to their trainer and irremediably dull-down once they are in the arena.

"He who sows the tempest will harvest the wind."
(René Bacharach, "Réponses équestres")

By using the Spanish walk any horse can learn a respectable passage: Spanish walk is the only exercise that allows the rider to free the horse's shoulders and to lift the neck sufficiently for passage.

The approach to Spanish walk: by touching with the whip the rider firstly teaches the jambette, until an ample gesture is achieved.

Alternative

A good passage can certainly be obtained from a trot or a piaffe, but only with horses that naturally tend to have expressive movements or that have a long suspension time in these two paces. Subjects selected for dressage competition have a basic trot whose cadence, elasticity and expression are often already halfway to a passage.

To really get to the heart of the subject we have to find an approach that allows us to give a correct passage to any horse. This is a whole different story.

Features of the passage

The passage does not result from either the flexing of the back and the haunches, nor the engagement of the hind legs. It is characterised by an increased suspension time which partly comes from the propelling of the hind legs, but also from the lifting of the shoulders.

The same is true for passage as it is for jumping: if the shoulders do not raise sufficiently to start with, the pushing of the hind legs remains without effect (refusal or fault).

How can we raise the shoulders? The only exercise through which we can give the shoulders the necessary freedom to lift is the Spanish walk. And this can be taught to even very ordinary horses by a skilled rider.

Progression from Spanish walk to passage

• Teach the horse the jambette (raising and stretching out one leg), firstly at halt to give ample extension (leg horizontal). Keep the head high for the extended and vertical brachio-cephalic muscles to pull the shoulder upwards.
• High hands. Associate the demi-arrêt on one rein with a touch of the whip on the corresponding leg.
• Then repeat the jambette at each stride, firstly on one side then on the other.
• Lastly, gradually combine the two front legs until a symmetrical Spanish walk is obtained that moves correctly forwards.

He then continues this under saddle.
Photos: Laurioux

- Repeat this work under saddle. The horse learns to raise its shoulders to give ample movement of the forelegs with a permanent desire to move forward. It should be noted that at this stage the walk tends to become more diagonal.
- Alternate with increasingly close transitions between Spanish walk and trot without any hesitation. At one point these two movements come close enough together to combine them. The horse often offers greater suspension time.
- After a few closer transitions the rider asks for a strike off to trot from Spanish walk whilst maintaining the aids for the latter (high hands, alternating demi-arrêts and if necessary touching with the whip at the shoulders).

The horse mixes the two a little clumsily at first but then the suspension time will be set up with increasing clarity as the transitions progress. In the end, the alternating of brief sequences of Spanish walk and piaffe just before moving into passage will lead the horse to express itself fully in this air.

If the rider knows the horse's needs he can develop these separately and then bring them together to achieve the target air: a true training strategy.

Horses with relatively inexpressive paces give very correct and even astonishing passages using this approach. This method also improves the passage of gifted horses, giving it greater height, roundness and cadence.

In conventional dressage circles, it is common to consider Spanish walk as non-classical - a circus trick that serves no purpose and that is vaguely frowned upon. To this can reply: giving a good Spanish walk to a horse is not easy and is therefore worthy of interest. What is classical is to manage to give a correct passage to any horse using gentle and intelligent methods.

The only precaution we would recommend is not to start the approach to ridden Spanish walk before having a good initial piaffe.

Conclusion

Considered as they should be (in other words as changes of balance) transitions, rein-back, piaffe and passage show that the raising of the base of the neck is the main key to an approach to collection.

It lightens the front end and allows us to produce useful transitions. It facilitates and justifies the bringing of the hind end under the horse's body for the piaffe. Through Spanish walk it leads to an increase in the movement of the shoulders leading to passage.

Again we must not consider a "low hand" as a panacea and understand that the hand is gentle and useful when it acts upwards, with a constant focus on the "descente de main" (lowering of the hand).

Past masters told us correctly that a good piaffe leads to a "gallant mouth". In his first method Baucher was right to say that combining the "cession de mâchoire" and the "raising of the neck" gave collection, even to mediocre horses - this is his famous reciprocal relationship.

When they achieve a good piaffe, all horses become light - but they need some serious aptitudes that are cleverly used. But all horses worked in légèreté can collect - even the most ordinary of them.

"The cherry on the cake" is good. *"The recipe for cherry cake"* is even better.

From Spanish walk to passage these two horses learnt to passage by combining Spanish walk and trot.
Photos: Slawik, Photo right: Laurioux

A SYSTEM
AND ITS EFFECTS

The Offical Training scale

Analysis of the official theory

Since this scale is intended to get the best out of all horses, we can study its application to an ordinary horse: unhelpful conformation, marked crookedness, modest paces, difficult temperament - in other words an average, normal horse. You are therefore starting the training of this horse just after it has been backed. (It accepts being ridden on the lunge in a natural attitude.)

Rhythm

You must start here, it is the priority objective in the scale.

• You shorten your reins with low hands: the horse goes above the bit and rushes - goodbye rhythm!
• You close your legs to put the horse forward: it holds back. You use your whip on it: it starts to rush again - goodbye rhythm!
• You put it on a circle: on one rein it does not turn very well and tends to hold back, on the other it leans inwards and rushes - goodbye rhythm!

• At canter: on one leg it canters quite well, on the other it tends to strike off on the wrong leg, disunite, etc. - goodbye rhythm!

All of which gives the unpleasant impression of someone who has to use a bike with bent wheels, an off-centre pedal block, seized handlebars and no brakes. What about rhythm? Perplexed, you think that the horse may need some initial education to the aids, that this will give you a way of reassuring your partner and have it understand you. Well unfortunately that is not possible! Rhythm first, because suppleness, contact and impulsion only come later on in the scale!

You decide to ask an instructor who is familiar with the mysteries of this scale.

He tells you that you have omitted a few technical preliminaries: lungeing the horse in side-reins, especially short if your horse tries to lift its nose. A double crank noseband, tightened as hard as possible will complete the system.

In the best case, after a few worrying attempts to evade, the horse will give in by becoming overbent in all three paces. For good measure, and to confirm this result, the instructor will have you do your ridden work in draw reins. You will be more inclined to be satisfied with this initial submission if you are also told: *"Good! Now the horse is round and has given its back!"* We can move on to the next part of the scale.

Suppleness

In reality, not only have you not solved any problems, you have in fact added one very major one: overbending. Overbent on itself, the neck is shortened, losing its lateral freedom, restricting the movement of the forelegs and putting the horse on the shoulders (without counting the physiological and psychological problems it causes as well).

According to its conformation, your horse will overbend either by avoiding taking a contact on the reins or by leaning heavily on the hand. But you are not meant to worry about this because the scale looks at contact after it has covered suppleness!

Concerning suppleness - with the naivety that comes from common sense, you ask your instructor: *"With a difficult contact and without the possibility of seriously bending the neck, how am I going to be able to supple my horse?"* And he will reply, unruffled: *"You must not bend the neck very much. The most important thing in suppling is the costal flexion."*

You will therefore learn how to energetically use your legs, then your spurs, with your leg on one side at the girth and with the other one behind the girth, to bend the horse and supple it throughout its body. You will ride like this for miles on circles seeking what your horse cannot give you since *"the costal flexion"* is an illusion. In addition, the impulsive ability of the legs is not yet on the training scale (schwung comes later and the concept of impulsion is nowhere to be found) and you will desensitise your horse to them.

Even though you ask for ever more *"leg yields"* it is not by using lateral work without any bend in the neck that you will manage to supple your horse. Jostled forwards by the legs and the spurs, asking it for more than it can give, your horse will often end up rushing its paces – especially since overbending puts it on the shoulders and the contact is far from perfect: loss of rhythm - back to square one!

Contact and schwung

Perplexed and sceptical, you ask your instructor how to get out of this difficult situation. He will answer *"Your horse is lacking contact and schwung, because it is not energetically engaging its hindquarters towards the centre of gravity"*. You will therefore learn to increase the number of regulatory *"half-halts"* – weighing heavily on your seat bones and pushing energetically with your legs onto *"low and active hands"*.

But the results are disappointing! Depending on your horse it will either hold back or rush for three main reasons:

• Being compressed between contradictory aids tenses and dulls the horse.
• Shortening of the bases and forwards movement are incompatible. Therefore: no increased engagement of the hind legs.
• The unavoidable backwards effect of your "low hands" increases overbending and puts the horse even more on the shoulders.

Things then go from bad to worse:

• Rhythm and suppleness are not improved due to a lack of relaxation, flexibility and balance.
• Depending on the horse, the contact may deteriorate with the horse absolutely refusing to stretch into the reins (a feeling that will be mistakenly called lightness), or the horse may just start to lean (which will make you believe that the horse is stretching into its reins).
• In terms of schwung, the paces will remain restricted and unexpressive. Denatured by the blocked spine, the walk will become lateral or will literally become an amble - what about rhythm?
• In terms of straightness you will be limited to doing the best you can to manage stiffness.
• As for collection - well, you had better get used to life without it.

In summary: lateral work will remain limited, laborious and useless, flying changes will be hazardous or impossible, collection will be excluded. (A passagey trot: perhaps. A piaffe: never.) And concerning the absolute priority given to rhythm: out of three paces, one will have been seriously denatured - the walk (a key pace).

At the end of the experience, and maybe even well before, you will be told: *"You will have to change your horse because this one is no good for dressage"* – and there you were thinking that dressage was for all horses!

This description is certainly no fantasy, nor is it malicious. It corresponds to technical and teaching realities that are considered unavoidable.

Overview

Those who consider this scale wonderful, know it by heart and stick to it; but those who try to understand it are a lot less enthusiastic.

Rhythm: what miracle makes it the source of everything? Rhythm can only result from work that sets up relaxation and flexibility (suppleness) in forwards movement. This therefore involves an initial education to the aids: the hands (contact) and the legs (impulsion). Rhythm cannot come first unless you have bought it with the horse - and naturally good paces are expensive. But that is business and not dressage.

Do we teach children classical dancing before they have the language (school of the aids), an upright stance (balance) and a minimum of physical education (suppleness)? Of course not!

Schwung: this is the energetic and vibrant gesture that prolongs the suspension time and gives expression to paces. Schwung is therefore synonymous with cadence. Horses that interest competition dressage circles already have this quality in their paces when they are foals. Unless you buy it with the horse (the prices go up another notch), schwung can only result from genuine collection. By training his horse to give a correct piaffe (through energetic transitions) then passage (often via Spanish walk), the rider will be able to cadence its paces and especially the trot. When correctly understood, collection is therefore not an end in itself, but is also a way of improving more average natural paces.

Straightness: whilst it is necessary for collection, it is above all something that is sought at an early stage, as well as being a permanent focus of all training. Indeed, how could

a young horse that is very crooked and tense have harmonious contact, suppleness and a regular rhythm without initially having acquired a significant degree of straightness by developing its lateral flexibility? Looking for straightness at such a late stage is the rather debatable privilege of riders who can pay for talented and easy horses (and the price continues to rise!).

Collection: considering it as a stage that requires specific and major resources (systematically looking for piaffe using coercive methods backed up by working in-hand), is the same as confusing collection and compression – and implicitly admitting to shortfalls in the preliminary training.

Collection is naturally developed in the end, but all of the horse's education must work towards it through the ongoing search for the best compromise between relaxation – balance – impulsion. Genuine collection requires extreme concentration of the horse's forces. This over-activity in slow motion, that is explosive by definition, can only be fully expressed under two conditions: the right balance and total relaxation. There is no correct schooling without correctly managing balance – but the term, although fundamental, does not appear at any point in this scale.

We would expect a dressage scale to give the most reliable approach through a succession of steps placed in the most logical order.

However this scale is often rather arbitrary. Simply looking at it with common sense reveals chronological errors, abusive amalgams and fundamental omissions such as the school of aids or balance.

Summary

The diagram overleaf shows a few modifications that we could make to this scale.

This diagram is not just pure theory - it corresponds to practice.

Combined with serious shortfalls and notable inconsistencies, the original scale's

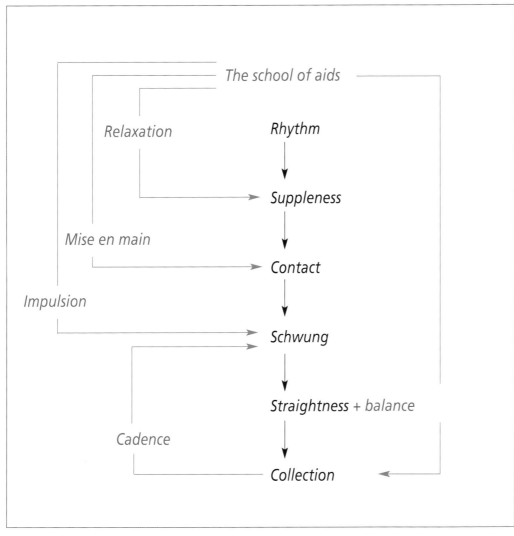

Examining the scale in dressage manuals reveals fundamental omissions and serious inconsistencies (supplemented in red).

requirements are more like an expeditive approach for gifted horses (aiming to satisfy the judges) rather than a genuine plan for dressage.

This is why the system often leads to an empirical approach based on constraint which eliminates the large majority of horses.

It would therefore be a good idea to technically review this approach to training, since in many ways it completely misses the point.

At the end of this review we will come back to a proposed alternative.

Dressage, Breeding and Business

History

To fully understand the issue it is necessary to see how this modern speciality called "competition dressage" has evolved. It all started in the 1920s and was intended to be the common basis for all equestrian disciplines.

In spectacular fashion, and within a few decades, dressage has moved from a confi-dential, high-society confrontation between enthusiasts from various schools (German, Nordic, Russian and Latin) to sponsorised, mediatised and globalised professionalism, completely dominated by Germany.

Why and how is this the case? After the First World War Gustav Rau, an eminent head of German horse breeding, laid down the following directive: for dressage, breeders must breed

> "... a horse that has all the characteristics of a schooled horse, right from the start."

In 50 years, through remarkable breeders and very strict selection, the objective had been achieved.

To which we can add many riders who are passionate, methodical and rigorous. Through the overbearing superiority of its breeding programme, Germany ended up with such a domination of the discipline that it logically imposed firstly its horses, then the training methods of its professionals on both riders and trainers, and finally its judgement criteria on the FEI.

The business and sporting success was so overwhelming that it led to a technical and commercial monopoly being set up. And we have to acknowledge this achievement - although there is one major reservation: in cultural terms, standardisation and one way of thinking always tends to be a sign of impoverishment and even regression.

Dressage and trainers

Nowadays and in all countries, rather than "training" their horses, dressage profession-als tend to cleverly "use" their extraordinary talent (perfect confirmation, fabulous paces and outstanding mental attitude) - naturally bought for astronomical sums.

Generally, progress in breeding, the explo-sion of budgets and the professionalisation of the discipline have led to the emergence of a new type of rider: "the dressage rider".

General Pierre Durand, Ecuyer en Chef of the Cadre Noir, then Director of the National School of Equitation at Saumur, after an international career in eventing and show jumping, wrote the following on this subject:

"In terms of its vocation, and anyway in terms of the spirit of its audiences, riding seen in the dressage arenas is a blend of modern sports riding and 'timeless' artistic riding. This dual vocation is where it comes unstuck; it neither manages to be a sport, nor an art."
"... Equestrian Art has been reduced to the clever application of a few simple processes, adapted to a well defined discipline and difficult to transpose to other equestrian disciplines. This means that we now see specialist show jumping riders and eventing riders (and even, dressage riders)."

The spirit, the letter and the foot notes

Mainly obsessed by results, modern dressage regularly confuses causes and effects. Consequently it fatally focuses on things that involve forcing the achievement of objectives. (With some of them even being a pure illusion: costal flexion, engagement of the hindquarters, etc.) This results in unsophisticated processes, authoritarian methods and lastly dogmas with detrimental consequences since they are contrary to the horse's nature. Three examples are quite good at summarising the distortions induced by this simplistic approach.

Mise en main

• Observation:
A schooled horse stabilises its neck by approaching its head to the vertical.

• Deduced approach:
As soon as it is lunged, the horse is placed on the vertical by using side reins. In the saddle, draw reins are used if necessary.

• Induced dogmas:
Not worrying about the mouth, and worrying very little about the neck since the main resistances are in the poll.
– low hands whatever happens
– never lift the neck using the hand.

• Detrimental consequences:
– hands acting backwards
– authoritarian, tightly shut nosebands
– overbent horses that are behind the bit and on the shoulders.

Suppleness and overall bend

• Observation:
The bend of a schooled horse exactly follows the curve that it is on.
• Deduced approach:
Maintaining the spine regularly bent from the poll to the tail by weighting the inside seat bone and using active legs: inside leg at the girth, outside leg behind.

• Induced dogmas:
– limiting bend in the neck
– focusing on maintaining costal flexion
– always weighting the seat to the inside of the bend.

• Detrimental consequences:
– fixed necks and blocked backs
– ambling walks and passagey trots
– permanent use of the legs which serves no purpose apart from dulling the horse
– seat used contrary to the laws of balance: used wrongly in half of the lateral work and in counter-canter, out of phase for canter strike offs and flying changes.

Balance and collection

• Observation:
In the piaffe, a symbol of collection, the horse moves energetically on the spot by engaging its active hind legs under its body.

• Deduced approach:
In all downward transitions, for halts and the rein back, use active legs to engage the hind legs towards the centre of gravity.

• Induced dogmas:
– the half-halt carried out by simultaneously using restraining and propulsive aids
– never acting with the hand unless energetically supported by the seat and the legs
– the more legs the better.

• Detrimental consequences:
– heavy, contradictory and purposeless use of the aids, which makes the horse inattentive to the legs and tense, and which increases overbending:
– In the end, compressed, dulled and over bent, the horse shuffles on its shoulders rather than piaffing.

• Overview
The rider's demands are so often contrary to realities in terms of anatomy, locomotion and balance, that they often lead to results that are the opposite of those being sought, as well as having a negative psychological impact.

These approaches inevitably generate a coercive and aggressive riding style, that must be compensated for by the natural talent of horses, and which cause an insidious distortion of the judging criteria.

Indeed the rules increasingly align with professional requirements, and the principles of Equestrian Art are constantly giving more ground under the pressure of the sector and its interests - in the name of business.

A few examples show how far off-track dressage competitions have strayed.

Mobility of the jaw

Until 1958, the FEI rules recommended that judges assess the relaxation and balance of horses by the mobility of their jaw.

> *"At all paces, slight mobility of the jaw, without nervousness, is a guarantee of submission and a harmonious distribution of forces."*

Since then, this very important article has been withdrawn and crank nosebands have become common fare - to everyone's general satisfaction.

Overbending

Noted as a serious fault by all masters in equestrian literature, overbending has now become a system. At the very *"highest levels"* riders are winning by presenting horses that are regularly overbent. They even openly promote this under the name of *"rollkur"*.

Gaits, airs and coefficients

Dressage tests and the coefficients in them tend, on one hand, to promote things that are mainly due to the aptitude of horses and the cleverness of riders and on the other hand, to marginalise or minimise anything that might put them in difficulty and reveal any serious faults in their training.

• Horses intended to have a career in "top level dressage" have naturally outstanding paces, including their walk - from the St Georges to the Grand Prix Special, extended walk, with long reins, is coefficient 2.

However, collection in this pace poses serious problems to most competitors. Tension and imbalance denature the collected walk and make it tend towards an amble - the walk work is reduced to a minute portion (St Georges, Intermediary II, Grand Prix and Grand Prix Special cumulated: on average walk only represents 11 to 12% of the points).

• The horses have spectacular trots and the tests indeed focus on this pace, increasing the number of medium and extended trots as well as half-passes. In the Grand Prix and the Grand Prix Special, long trot half-passes are coefficient 2.

• The horses have very big canters and flying changes do not cause many problems for riders who generally manage to execute them - the tests include diagonals with four, three, two-beat and tempi flying changes that are coefficient 2; in the same way as half-passes to the centre line and pirouettes.

N.B.: We could also note that from a utilitarian point of view, tempi changes serve no purpose. They are an end in themselves, seriously debatable since they deteriorate the pace by producing a sort of "ambling canter" – denounced by certain authors.

"Changing leg one after another is an ambled pace, like that of the giraffe, and we would not consider it worthy of mentioning further if so much fuss had not been made about it..." *(Louis Seeger, Serious Warning to Germany's riders)*

• Due to major equestrian faults, passages are often laborious or jerky, piaffes are often shuffling or imitations - although these classical airs are irreplaceable tests of collection they remain coefficient 1. A horse can therefore win at "top level" with disastrous collected paces.

• As proof of incorrect training that is detrimental to the horse, any deterioration of the horse's locomotion should be unacceptable. And yet an impressive list of winners have done so with "ambled walks" instead of collected walk, and "passagey trots" instead of collected trot.

What can we conclude? Obviously these are rather indulgent rules tailored to an objective.

Overbending is now the rule:
At the "highest level" people are winning on horses that are regularly overbent. These pictures were taken in 2004 at the Athens Olympic Games and at international dressage competitions. Photos: Toffi

Redefining the piaffe

The piaffe, the ultimate in collection and out-standing proof of balance and impulsion, is most often poorly executed or an imitation. Not only does this not stop people from winning, but also the official texts have insidious-ly shifted the definition of this classical air to better correspond to what is happening in the arena.

As proof of this, simply compare the illus-trations in the 1987 and 1997 editions of Book 2.

• 1987 edition
The drawing, probably inspired by a photo of Otto Lörke, shows an irreproachable piaffe. Hands slightly raised, the rider presents a horse which, with its poll open and the highest point, piaffes high in front, flexes its back, low-ers its haunches and flexes its hindquarters well under its body.

• 1997 edition
The drawing shows a rider with low hands, presenting a "fashionable" piaffe: the head is vertical and the poll is not the highest point of the neck.

The horse is distinctly on its shoulders and without any elevation in its movement. The haunches are not lowered because the hind-quarters are engaged without flexing.

This is an accurate representation of the "pseudo-piaffe", the art of putting the horse on its shoulders, shown so often by dressage riders.

This is how the official authorities endorse the profession: by side-tracking equestrian cul-ture and institutionalising a corrupted ap-proach to training. All of which does not stop the FEI rules from continuing to remind peo-ple that their vocation is to:

"Preserve equestrian art from any changes that it may be exposed to and preserve it in the purity of its principles to pass it on intact to future generations." (Article 419)

The comparison of illustrations of the 1987 (on the left) and 1997 (on the right) editions of Book 2 of the Dressage Manuals, which have been redrawn here, show to what extent the rules are aligned with what is happening in the arena.

This is surreal!

There is only one conclusion to make: whilst horses have improved incredibly in terms of quality, at the same time equestrian principles and training methods have tragically re-gressed. When confronted with such protests, people in this sports-business will always fall back on their supreme argument: "It must be the best system- it always wins in the dressage arena." Impossible to deny, but we can still make a few observations:

• The system manages the selection of horses and keeps the best for itself, it trains the teachers and the trainers, it writes the rules and controls the judges, it has all media and financial resources – how could it not domi-nate the discipline?
• Dressage competition is subjective by nature since it depends on a human judgement. Sub-ject to manipulation, it has generated an absolute monopoly of one single idea.
As opposed to this, in eventing and show jumping, more objective disciplines because they above all depend on the jump and the stopwatch, there is no overwhelming domi-nation and the results are full of diversity.
• The results are there, but at what price? How do the horses contribute to this out-standing success?

The proportion of horses that the system irremediably ruins in the first years of their "use" is enormous. Official authorities claim not to have figures on the subject. We must use private sources. For example, a study pre-sented at Giessen in 1977 by Dr H. Gutekunst under the guidance of Professor Dr. J. Nassal gave the following information:

• Statistics from the Federal Property Insur-ance Company concerning saddle horses in the Republic of Germany between 1971 and 1974 study covering 6,464 cases.
• Average usage of saddle and competition horses: 5.54 years.
• Average age of retirement: between 8 and 9 years.

- Main causes of retirement: problems with the locomotor system (premature wearing due to early and irregular usage).
- In the age group from 5 to 12 years old: 76.43% of damage, 65.64% of deaths, 74.56% of emergency euthanasia, 77.81% of retirement for definitive loss of aptitude.

It is increasingly frequent for personalities, including some vets, to raise a voice of concern - which remains without effect for the time being. It would be useful for the competent authorities to produce statistics over the past 20 or 30 years since there is a persistent rumour that is going around that says that dressage horses have an even shorter average life.

This is probably what Nuno Oliveira was talking about when he wrote:

"What we must do is work in légèreté. Anything else is a massacre of innocents."
(M. Henriquet, Correspondence with Nuno Oliveira)

Conclusion

Titles and medals are not enough to measure the value of a system, however predominant it is. If we made a world ranking of restaurants, McDonald's would come out on top. And yet it is certainly not a benchmark for healthy eating and even less a place for gastronomic traditions. By developing without the safeguards of judiciously designed events and healthy judgement criteria, the professionalisation of dressage has caused a vicious circle:

- The better the horses, the higher their prices and the more they have to be profitable
- ...meaning they are used earlier and in more abusive ways.
- But the more the horses are stressed, the more the associated professions prosper: specialist vets, osteopaths, acupuncturists, horse whisperers etc.

- ...and the more we see illicit treatments and doping scandals.
- The lower their life expectancy, the more horses are sold by breeders.
- The better the aptitude and strength of sports horses... the more their breeding selection improves.
- Which improves the next generation ... and so on.

The wheel turns ever faster. It is make or break! In an increasingly competitive and "disposable" society, the only things that count are results. "Man's noblest conquest" is therefore reduced to an investment, without any qualms.

Whilst with characteristic cynicism the business finds this a very profitable arrangement, these increasingly high performance horses pay a high price and training loses its soul and its educational virtues. If we believe that equestrian sport has the main duty of protecting the horse, and that dressage has a key educational role, it would be a good idea to moderate any tendency for self-satisfaction.

As the sole benchmark for dressage training, competition dressage has a major influence on the world equestrian scene. It smoothes out any differences and drags everything downwards. To varying extents, but without exception, the twisted truths of modern dressage seriously pollute all of Europe's major schools. If it does not manage to radically turn around this trend, competition dressage will be condemned to becoming a speciality with business objectives, generating its own rules, introspective, cut off from other disciplines and from equestrian culture and therefore unable to train valid teachers.

As a common basis for all equestrian disciplines, dressage is the basis for the training of all riders. However because of the system, teachers are trained in a training approach limited to the quest for results in "dressage competitions". This blinkered vision is easy to impose in our times when people tend to con-

fuse everything - confusing results and basics, confusing advertising and truth, confusing information and culture. This is a shame because the skill and day-to-day life of an instructor is much more to do with improving any horse and all riders, rather than searching for something special with which they can "get results".

Riding teachers are often reduced to using hollow, meaningless words with vague explanations, irrefutable and righteous attitudes in order to protect themselves. All of which produces an authoritarian, off-putting and unstructured teaching approach because the content is so poor.

Consequently, with a lack of technical, teaching and cultural resources required to produce skilled teachers who feel confident, many horses are ruined and many riders are put off - with the most clear-thinking of them prematurely abandoning the profession.

Those riders who are not obsessed with competition, or who do not have the resources to buy a "dressage horse", give up riding or desperately seek an alternative. This is how, by always going further from its classical roots, conventional dressage indirectly promotes parallel riding approaches. Dressage enthusiasts increasingly turn to so-called "baroque", "Spanish" or "Portuguese" equitation, all of which intend to be classical.

Looking at them carefully, whilst the clothing, tack, types and attitudes of the horses are different, the principles and training methods do not vary significantly. A Louis XV costume does not make an Ecuyer any more than a cassock makes a monk. While the nostalgia and folklore is charming, and certainly looks as nice as a dressage outfit, it does not do much to progress the art of riding.

"Classical or not Classical?"

That is the question. This term has been so over-used that we should look into its deep-rooted meaning. This rather flattering adjective implies an historical reference which is rather austere, but which automatically gives legitimacy and respectability to anyone who adopts it: each person has their own way of being classical:

• Official dressage and competition dressage claim a classical heritage that justifies their monopoly on training teachers and on managing competition dressage.
• A host of riders link classical riding with the use of so-called "baroque" breeds, to the exclusion of any other.
• Because the equipment was used in the 17th and 18th centuries, many people think they are classical if they use pillars, bullfighting saddles and long-branched curb bits.
• Lastly, others want to be classical by obstinately refusing to jump the slightest jump and instead focusing on "croupades", "balotades" and other "caprioles".

Is it enough to be a specialist in the minuet to be defined as a "classical dancer"? However nice and respectable they are, these fashionable trends are restrictive and outdated.

Obviously, classicism is not a speciality. It cannot be reduced to conservatism, nor should we forget the positive contribution of modern and sports riding. In order to gain a clear idea in this respect, we can put dressage in its historical perspective by looking at how riding has changed over the past centuries and the innovations that have marked its development and made it progress.

Dressage in history

The Middle Ages

Generally this is a dark period for the horse. Riding was limited to a warlike, empirical and often cruel use of the horse based on impressive bridles and terrifying spurs.

The Italian Renaissance

In the 15th century, a war of succession to the kingdom of Naples opposed two pretenders and two approaches:

• The cavalry of Charles VIII, of medieval type, focusing on the power of force... and that of Ferdinand of Aragon, riding in a "ginetta" style: a riding approach that found its roots when conquering back land from the Moors and in bullfighting, based on speed and agility. The French were defeated and the Iberian horse went on to inspire a decisive equestrian revolution.

Under the authority of Federico Grisone, the Academy of Naples acquired a reputation that attracted riders from throughout Europe.

• Grisone
In 1550 he published the first equestrain treatise of the modern era: *Gli Ordinii di cavalcare.* In it he gives an initial definition of the mise en main:

"If the horse comes on the bit, with its nose coming to the vertical whilst extending its neck, it will not only have a more frank contact, but it will also hold its neck more firmly, without ever changing its position and with a gentle contact that accompanies the hand accommodating the bit with its mouth, chewing it just like it has always been used to it: and whatever the quality of the horse, good or bad, it will always therefore be forwards and elegant and appear to be perfect."

• Pignatelli
A disciple of Grisone and Fiaschi, he first put forward the idea of not determining the mise en main through physical restriction, and therefore using a simplified bit, the same one for all horses.

Salomon de la Broue explains this in his *Precepts of French Equitation* (1594):

"... since he made the horses so obedient, handling them so correctly with such beautiful airs, that we saw them at his school, without using any other bits than an ordinary canon with a common cavesson, his rules and his experience had a lot more effect than the approach of all others who work with all the artifices, a host of bridles and a few special secrets that are most often useless, that they still use when they are missing the most beautiful and most important resources of their art."

The gentler and simplified Pignatel bit was used until the end of the 18th century.

• William Cavendish
The first Duke of Newcastle (1592 – 1676), whilst he unfortunately invented draw reins, challenged the use of double pillars, generally attributed to Pluvinel and used to collect the horse. As opposed to this he recommended the single pillar to supple the horse on a circle on one or two tracks. Newcastle favoured the use of the cavesson and the bridoon for the basic education of a young horse.

• François Robichon de La Guérinière (1688 – 1751)
He freed the horse from the constraint of the single pillar, developing lunge work and denying the utility of any schooling aids. He developed the shoulder-in, intended to balance and supple the horse on a straight line. He defined the pair: demi-arrêt – descente de main – leaving the horse freedom and testing the horse's balance.

l'Épaule en Dedans.

A lesson in shoulder-in given by La Guérinière.

- Louis Cazeau de Nestier (1684 – 1754)

The favourite ecuyer of Louis XV and member of the Versailles school, he will be remembered for recommending the use of a short-branched curb bit combined with a snaffle bit: "the Nestier bit".

- François Baucher (1796 – 1873)

He had amazing intuition that made him an ethologist and an osteopath before his time. He developed preparatory in-hand work including a programme of flexions (jaw, neck, poll) and mobilisations (haunches around the shoulders, shoulders around the haunches) enabling the horse to be collected without using pillars or training aids.

He discovered that légèreté is not only the happy consequence of collection, but it can be the cause. In his second manner, presented by Faverot de Kerbrech, he recommends the separate use of the aids "hand without legs, legs without hand" and the raising of the neck. Presenting himself in the circus where he had to surprise a crowd of laymen, Baucher invented a large number of "new airs" of debatable utility and taste, including the famous tempi changes.

- Federigo Caprilli (1867 – 1907)

This young cavalry officer, who died when 39 years old, revolutionised equestrian sport and saved horses from a veritable torture by in-

This way of jumping, which was torture for horses, was used until the 1920's.
Cavalry officer Federico Caprilli (below) invented the new way of leaning forwards in equilibrium for jumping.

venting the equilibrium jumping style. With the open mind and intuition that are the mark of a genius, he discovered what is today taken as obvious: in jumping, by weighting the stirrups, the rider uses his torso like the horse uses its head and neck to balance. In other words: complying with balance and locomotion or even the nature of the horse, the best of all guides.

- Horse whisperers

This "new equestrian wave" is prospering due to the insufficiency and excess of official dressage. Carried by a strong fashionable trend and supported by the contribution of ethology, these "behaviourist" trainers offer non-violent domination, which corresponds to the needs of neophytes and a basic use of the horse. Their success once again shows the benefits that riding can get from in-depth knowledge of the nature of the horse.

Conclusion

There is a common thread throughout this brief overview of the history of riding: Equestrian Art has progressed every time it has substituted intelligence for force – abolishing instruments of coercion and simplifying material resources, searching for causes instead of focusing on their

effects, getting ever closer to identifying the deep-rooted nature of the horse.

From this point, it appears that the adjective "classical" is used too often when that of "typical", "traditional" or "conventional" would be amply sufficient. In riding, classicism is a state of mind that is without a period, without boundaries and without specialities - a requirement that is both ethical and aesthetic, used to serve Equestrian Art. It involves the rejection of easy options that the horse pays for in an ongoing search for efficiency and economy of resources. It distances itself from flashy effects and focuses on the purity of gaits and airs, which are intended to sublimate the horse and guarantee its long life.

Put in its historical context, what contribution has competition dressage made to the Equestrian cause?

- The systematic use of coercive means (side reins and other training aids, crank nosebands).
- Basic training faults established as a system (overbending, etc.).
- Frequent deterioration in locomotion (ambled walk and passagey trot).
- Failure in terms of harmony (working by force) and in terms of balance (imitation piaffe).
- The promotion of extended gaits and flying changes at canter, combined with an insidious devaluing of collection.
- The premature and authoritarian use of the horse's aptitudes that damages its physical integrity and shortens its life.

In spite of having considerable and unprecedented talent in terms of horses (with their outstanding aptitudes) and in terms of people (specialised professionals) official dressage is undeniably leading to the regression of Equestrian Art. This is completely at odds with the previously described historical process. Dressage is no longer classical.

PROPOSING A CLASSICAL ALTERNATIVE

The Schooling
of Légèreté

This school has the founding principle of
absolute respect of the horse. As a humorist
once said: "It goes without saying, but it's
even better if we say it". It takes its inspiration from the masters who have contributed
to this equestrian philosophy: Xenophon,
Fiaschi, La Broue, Pluvinel, La Guérinière,
Dupaty de Clan, Hünersdorf, Baucher, Raabe,
L'hotte, Faverot de Kerbrech and Beudant,
Oliveria etc.

Légèreté is not a declaration of intent of
a poetic or esoteric nature but a philosophy
bringing together clear, effective and meas-
urable equestrian concepts. It excludes any
use of force or coercive artificial aids, but
includes all types of horse and takes an
interest in all equestrian disciplines.

This school is based on in-depth knowledge of the horse and is ready to re-analyse
and improve itself with all types of progress
in this respect (anatomy, physiology, locomotion, balance, psychology, ethology).

Lastly it has the aim of getting the best
from the horse and fulfilling the rider
through the constant search for efficiency
via the minimum use of means.

Photo: Slawik

The concept of légèreté excludes any use of force
*or coercive artificial aids, but includes
all types of horses and takes an interest
in all equestrian disciplines.
(Quiela, 7 year old Lusitano stallion)
Photos: Laurioux*

Training scale

A training scale cannot claim to have all the answers. However it must at least give a general framework, a logical approach and reliable points of reference. The training scale that is proposed here results from points that have been explained and proven in the previous chapters.

The figure below shows:
• The order of the main stages to be complied with in the training approach.
• The order of priorities to be re-established when the rider encounters any difficulties.

Core principle: respect of the horse.

This is the heart and the soul of this approach. It rejects any approach involving unconditional submission through constraint and requires the search for obedience through dialogue.

This dialogue requires the learning of a language: the school of aids.

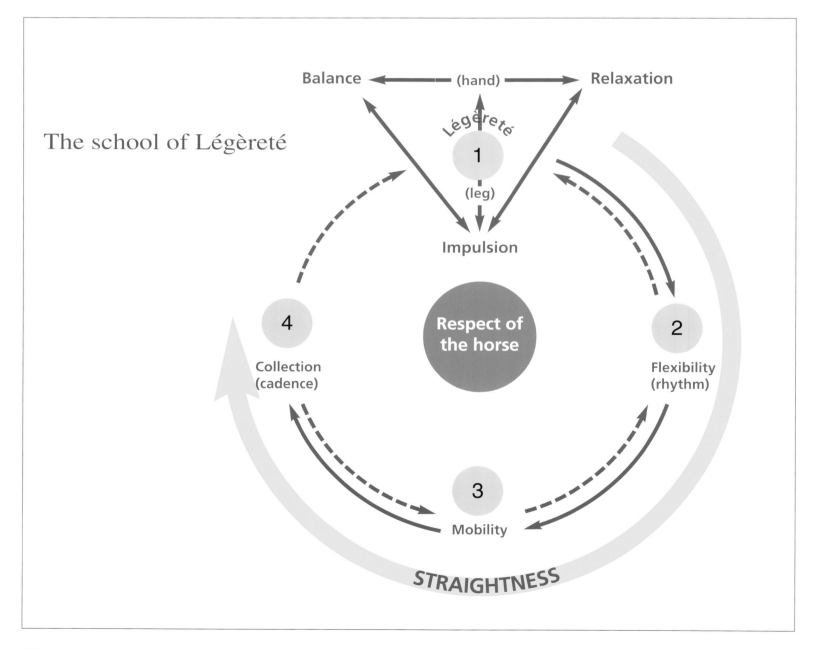

The school of Légèreté

Balance ← (hand) → Relaxation

Légèreté

1

(leg)

Impulsion

4
Collection (cadence)

Respect of the horse

2
Flexibility (rhythm)

3
Mobility

STRAIGHTNESS

Step No. 1: initial *légèreté*

After having established obedience to the voice and used basic gymnastic exercises through work on the lunge, the rider must put his horse in the basic school of aids: teaching the meaning of the signals given by the hands, the legs and the seat.

From simple to more complex, from words to sentences, he teaches the aids by separating them as far as possible from one another (*"hands without legs, legs without hands"*) firstly by foot, then in the saddle; at halt then progressing to walk. As soon as possible he will validate what has been learned at trot and canter.

Légèreté supposes simultaneously setting up three essential and inseparable elements: relaxation – balance – impulsion.

Relaxation

This is a priority because without relaxation nothing constructive happens. The best way for a rider to gain a horse's attention, while it is relaxed and permeable is by mobilising the lower jaw and the tongue (cession de mâchoire).

Relaxation therefore results from the hand and only the hand, naturally in a general climate of trust.

Balance

A horse that leans on the hand puts itself on the forehand and tenses its jaw. It is therefore by sufficiently raising the neck that the rider can obtain the *cession de mâchoire.*

Insufficient balance means no relaxation, and vice versa. In the end, the hand has the combined role of establishing or re-establishing the balance – relaxation pairing (2) since it alone can determine the position of the forehand and the *cession de mâchoire.*

Lightness to the hand is fundamental.

Impulsion

It is by giving the lesson of the leg by the intelligent use of the whip that the rider makes the horse totally and immediately responsive to the slightest pressure of the legs. He makes him *"light to the leg"*. No impulsion, no equitation.

Without impulsion, relaxation and balance go hand in hand with inertia and laziness.

Conversely, when developed in tension and imbalance, impulsion only causes disorder or panic. Continuing to work a horse with resistances on the pretext of impulsion, leads to mediocre results and excessive wear.

Lightness to the hand and lightness to the legs are therefore closely linked. As far as possible the rider must develop one within the limits set by maintaining the other.

Step No. 2: flexibility

When a horse gives its mouth, it relaxes and becomes permeable to the hand. It allows the rider to bend the neck as required. By developing total lateral flexibility of the neck, the rider determines its degree of extension, supples the whole spine and reduces crookedness.

The horse works on curves: circles, figures of eight, serpentines in true bend and counter-bend. The rider then controls the horse's shoulders and is able to straighten the horse as required.

When the horse resists the bend, ask for a *cession de mâchoire* by slowing to walk or stopping if necessary…before re-establishing the lateral bend and starting to work again:

"Position precedes the action." *(Baucher)*

Resulting effect: the more the horse becomes flexible, the more it can maintain *légèreté* in forwards movement and the more it cadences its paces.

Step No. 3: mobility

Having a relaxed, forward and flexible horse allows the rider to push its overall gymnastic exercises even further and improve the control of its balance.

Through lateral work and transitions the horse improves in mobility. The correct use of lateral work gives the horse complete mobility in every direction: around the shoulders, around the haunches, on oblique lines and in every type of position (shoulder-in, counter shoulder-in, travers, renvers, half-pass). This allows the rider to change the horse's balance as he wants towards one particular shoulder or haunch, towards one lateral pair or the other.

Systematic work on transitions, in the paces and between paces improves the horse's longitudinal mobility and the horse yields even more to the rider's aids. Striking off to trot or canter from halt or rein-back are all tests of impulsion (lightness to the legs). Coming back to walk or halt and rein-back from trot and lastly canter are all tests of balance (lightness to the hand).

If the horse shows resistances: re-establish relaxation and flexibility by asking for a *cession de mâchoire* and lateral flexion or restore impulsion by a lesson to the leg before repeating the exercise in question.

Resulting effect: the more mobility the horse has in every direction the more it gives its haunches and gains in general flexibility, balance and lightness to the aids.

Step No. 4: collection

Collection is created by pushing longitudinal mobility to its ultimate degree. A horse capable of frequent and repeated transitions between trot and rein back over a few strides without any hesitation and without resistance has all it needs to start approaching the piaffe: the very essence of collection.

Raising the withers by transferring weight to its haunches and reining back (lightness to the hand) whilst remaining ready to move quickly forward (lightness to the legs), the horse may diagonalise a few strides whilst imperceptibly moving forwards. The rider will gradually develop the piaffe on this basis, in line with the principle of *"hands without legs, legs without hand"*. By close transitions between the piaffe and trot, many horses will give passage and, if necessary, transitions between Spanish walk and trot will obtain it from any horse and improve it in every case.

Once he approaches collection the rider will be able to cadence and stylise the paces and give them expression that they do not naturally have.

Result and effect: through greater impulsion, and by definition a state of unstable balance, a true piaffe gives the horse extreme mobility.

In the end, collection enhances and expresses the results of *légèreté*.

> *Légèreté* is therefore both the source of collection and its consequence – everything comes from it and everything leads back to it.

Straightness

Without straightness, the horse does not give itself fully. It is sought from the very start of training and is continually perfected at each of its stages:

1. A horse which gives a *cession de mâchoire* when asked by the right rein and left rein, is on the road to straightness.

2. A horse which accepts full lateral flexion on both sides, increases the symmetry of the movement of its spine and has basic straightness.

3. A horse shows that it has symmetry in terms of its capabilities, a superior sign of straightness, when it can transition between turning the haunches around the shoulders and the shoulders around the haunches, as well as between lateral movements on the straight line, as easily on both reins either bent to the inside or the outside.

4. The piaffe or passage in shoulder-in is both a test of straightness and a way of perfecting the symmetry of the movement in these airs.

> Like légèreté, straightness is an everyday quest for perfection that, by definition, is never totally complete.

Ecole de Légèreté

Under the name of "The School of Légèreté" this concept and logo have been legally patented in Germany, under the number 306080086 with the "Deutscher Patent and Markenamts". For more information on instructor training in the "School of Légèreté" either as students or auditors, please refer to the internet site www.philppekarl.com

Epilogue

To finish this book I wanted to pay tribute to my students. They have all proven a passion for equitation, which is only equalled by their love of the horse.

Since I could never include them all, I have chosen to focus on one exemplary representative in the person of Wibke Kühl and her horse Moses. Wibke celebrated her twentieth birthday in 2003 during a training course on my premises. For a whole year, this relatively inexperienced, but intelligent, methodical and passionate rider worked her horse under my guidance.

With a Haflinger dam and a Holsteiner sire, Moses (10 years old in 2003) is 1m52 high, stockily built, very willing, but mischievous and quite stubborn. He had an aptitude for jumping but very mediocre natural paces.

When he arrived he had a few notions of lateral work at walk and trot but tended to quickly overbend and rush on the forehand.

Moses never worked more than 45 minutes to 1 hour a day and jumped once a week. No training aids were ever used, but all flexions in hand and under saddle as well as all classical movements were studied. Personally I only rode him two or three times to assess his progress.

When Wibke left in December 2003, Moses was capable of the following either in a snaffle bridle or a double bridle:

• Modest extensions due to his natural paces...
• Comprehensive lateral work at all three paces.
• Correct isolated flying changes that were starting to come closer together...
• A remarkable piaffe: a lot of energy, the poll the highest point, haunches low and flexed, strong hindquarters under his body.
• A good Spanish walk.
• A passage that resulted from the Spanish walk that was not particularly expressive but very regular.
• Good transitions between piaffe and passage and vice versa.
• Jumping 1m20 to 1m30 with good style.
• And all of this with light aids and good humour together with a few "circus tricks".

Both of them proved that through légèreté, a high level of training can be achieved by a large number of people. Whilst talent remains a considerable advantage, above all it requires correct methods and enthusiasm.

Thank you to everyone.

"I have learnt a lot from my master;
 I have learnt more from my colleagues;
 I have learnt even more from my disciples."

(Proverb from past Rabbis, 1629)

Philippe Karl, March 2006

Wibke Kühl and Moses:
After one year of training with the "School of Légèreté", Moses shows a remarkable piaffe, a very regular passage and good Spanish walk. In addition he has good jumping style over jumps from 1m20 to 1m30.

BIBLIOGRAPHY

Philippe Karl on video:

The school of aids, vol. 1
The school of gymnastics, vol. 2
The school of dance, vol. 3
One year on, vol. 4

Production: Thomas Vogel

GLOSSARY

1. *Légereté:*

A horse that is light to the hand is one that, on half-released reins, mobilizes its tongue and lower jaw in a movement much like swallowing (producing saliva). The horse is said to "taste its bit".

When properly understood, lightness to the hand cannot be boiled down to the eventual happy consequence of collection. It is above all a training philosophy, an educational method that is as gentle as it is effective because it is natural. It teaches the horse the language of the aids and allows a rider to relax, balance and supple any horse.

Each attitude and each exercise, from the most basic through to the most complex, is prepared then validated by a *cession de mâchoire*.

Légereté is also applied to a horse that is light to the legs (see *descente de jambes*)

2. Cession de mâchoire:

Since the horse's mouth receives the action of the hand, it is the mouth that the rider must persuade and have yield from the outset. The horse displays its agreement to talk with the hand by softly mobilising its tongue and lower jaw. When the horse "tastes" its bits in this way, this allows the rider to ask for variations in attitudes in the following order: lateral neck flexions, extension of the neck and poll flexion.

3. Demi-arrêt and Descente de main:

As described by La Guérinière and Baucher (2nd manner), the *demi-arrêt* involves the upwards action of the hand without the slightest backwards action. Its effect is to rebalance the horse by raising the neck and lightening the contact (*cession de mâchoire*)

When only the hand acts, the *demi-arrêt* must not change the speed within the horse's pace. If accompanied by the rider's shoulders it should cause the horse to slow its pace.

The legs are only combined with a *demi-arrêt* to collect the horse (collected halt, piaffe, canter on the haunches)

Having acted upwards (with the fingers closing on the reins) the hand will naturally release by lowering (and opening the fingers): this is the *descente de main*. It serves to validate the operation with the horse maintaining its attitude and balance on released reins... confirmed by the cession de *mâchoire*

4. Mise en main:

This is a methodological approach to the action of the hand and to the gymnastic progression intended to position the front end in the following order: *cession de mâchoire* and raising of the neck then lateral flexions of the neck and its extension and lastly poll flexion. This correct approach to the mise en main will lead to *ramener*, or in other words the combined maximum raising of the neck, poll flexion and *cession de mâchoire*

5. Descente de jambes:

A horse has impulsion if it responds immediately and generously to the slightest pressure of the legs and maintains this activity without them needing to be used again (legs released and draped): this is then called the *descente de jambes.*

The best test of relaxation, balance and impulsion in a given exercise or air involves it being executed in a *descente d'aides* (hands and legs simply in contact)

6. Effet d'ensemble:

A powerful way of dominating a horse developed by the innovative genius of Baucher and which enables the instant cancelling out of any evasion. It is only applicable to a horse that has previously been educated to the aids (*mise en main* and impulsion having already been acquired)

The *effet d'ensemble* is taught in stages:

- first at halt, it involves fixing the hand and squeezing the fingers, whilst gradually applying the legs, then the spurs at the girth (in front of the position intended to put the horse forwards). Remaining in place, the horse tenses its abdominal area and rounds its back. Contracting the underneck muscles, it flexes the poll and lowers the head to give a *cession de mâchoire* - the fingers then the legs release immediately.

- once obtained at halt, the *effet d'ensemble* is then applied at walk, at trot and then at canter.

- once confirmed in all three paces, the *effet d'ensemble* allows the horse to be put "on the aids" simply by applying pressure with the spurs at the girth, without interrupting the horse's work (returning to a *descentes des aides*)

Most horses can reach a high level of schooling without using the *effet d'ensemble*. But there are many horses with difficult conformation or temperament that would be impossible to completely school without it.

The *effet d'ensemble* is only for very experienced riders.

Contrary to the claims of certain simplistic and fashionable amalgams, the *effet d'ensemble* has absolutely nothing in common with the system that involves compressing and overbending the horse between the legs which push and hands which pull.